Oceania Entrepreneurship

Vanessa Ratten
Editor

Oceania Entrepreneurship

palgrave
macmillan

Editor
Vanessa Ratten
La Trobe University
Melbourne, VIC, Australia

ISBN 978-981-16-7340-5 ISBN 978-981-16-7341-2 (eBook)
https://doi.org/10.1007/978-981-16-7341-2

Cover illustration: Valentin Valkov/Alamy Stock

This Palgrave Macmillan imprint is published by the registered company Springer Nature Singapore Pte Ltd.
The registered company address is: 152 Beach Road, #21-01/04 Gateway East, Singapore 189721, Singapore

Acknowledgements

Editing this book has been an arduous journey but rewarding task. Thus, it has been most gratifying to complete the book due to the high level of scholarship embedded in each chapter. My sincere thanks to Vishal Daryanomel for his support with this book. My gratitude goes to my family—Kaye, David, Stuart, Hamish, Tomomi and Sakura. My family has wholeheartedly supported my academic career. My mum—Kaye Ratten—inspired me to pursue this research project due to her love for entrepreneurship, history and travelling. This book would not have been possible without her support and encouragement. It has been a pleasure to edit this book due to the interesting entrepreneurial behaviour evident in the Oceania region. I have long been fascinated by the differences in entrepreneurial activity across Oceania. It is clear that economic growth is not the result of government policies alone but also requires the input of others including business owners, citizens and the community. While there is a tendency to point to entrepreneurship as an urban-level phenomenon, it also occurs in regional and rural areas. As an academic teaching and researching entrepreneurship, I am adamant that new contexts need to be explored. This means not generalizing entrepreneurship as something that occurs in the same way but rather acknowledging the country contexts. Thus, entrepreneurial activity in Oceania should not be overlooked. Entrepreneurship varies in its dimensions and meanings. This means it is important to make Oceania entrepreneurship more prominent in the academic community.

Contents

List of Contributors

Safiya Mukhtar Alshibani College of Business and Administration, Princess Nourah Bint Abdulrahman University, Riyadh, Saudi Arabia;
The University of Western Australia, Perth, Australia

Dave Crick Telfer School of Management, University of Ottawa, Ottawa, ON, Canada

James M. Crick School of Business and Economics, Loughborough University, Loughborough, UK

Ingebjorg Kristoffersen The University of Western Australia, Perth, Australia

Vanessa Ratten La Trobe University, Melbourne, VIC, Australia

Esha Thukral Department of Management, Sport and Tourism, La Trobe Business School, La Trobe University, Melbourne, VIC, Australia

Thierry Volery Zurich University of Applied Sciences—ZHAW, Winterthur, Switzerland;
The University of Western Australia, Perth, Australia

List of Figures

List of Tables

CHAPTER 1

Oceania Entrepreneurship: A Future Research Agenda

Vanessa Ratten

Introduction

Entrepreneurship has emerged as a key agenda item for all of Oceania's countries' economic and social policymakers. Consistent with this focus is an effort to go more into developing entrepreneurial activity. This is due to entrepreneurship being regarded as a strategic source of economic growth (Ratten & Jones, 2021). This emphasis on entrepreneurship in Oceania has not always been the case as other forms of economic activity such as internationalisation were given priority. Thus, attention was placed on other business activities such as exporting instead of entrepreneurship. The advent of the knowledge economy in the early 2000s changed this due to the increase in startup activity. As a result, the development of small business was re-emphasised and high-growth ventures were given

V. Ratten (✉)
La Trobe University, Melbourne, Australia
e-mail: v.ratten@latrobe.edu.au

V. Ratten (ed.), *Oceania Entrepreneurship*,
https://doi.org/10.1007/978-981-16-7341-2_1

priority in economic policy debates. This new economic period has been referred to as the entrepreneurial economy as innovation, risk-taking and futuristic thinking are valued.

Oceania is a geographic region that includes these countries: Australia, Micronesia, Fiji, Kiribati, Marshall Islands, Nauru, New Zealand, Palau, Papua New Guinea, Samoa, Solomon Islands, Tonga, Tuvalu and Vanuatu. There is a diverse range of countries in Oceania in terms of size, population and economic growth rates. The area of Oceania was named because most countries surround the Pacific Ocean. The largest country by landmass and population in Oceania is Australia. Oceania is divided into four main parts: Australasia, Melanesia, Micronesia and Polynesia. Sometimes Australia is referred to as a continent but when used with the term Oceania it also includes the other islands in the area. The highest mountain in Oceania is Mount Cook in New Zealand but the area of Oceania generally is more flatter than other continents. There is a diverse range of flora and fauna in Oceania with rainforests and deserts existing in parts. Most of the pacific islands have a tropical rainforest form of vegetation. The climate is mostly warm except for parts of Australia and New Zealand where there is snow. Oceania as a region was explored by numerous Europeans who colonised many of the countries.

There is now a growing body of literature exploring entrepreneurship in Oceania. This means a diverse range of issues is included within this umbrella term. The majority of entrepreneurship research is premised on North American and European perspectives so new approaches are required (Ferreira et al., 2017a). Thus, I suggest research on Oceania entrepreneurship can encourage greater reflexivity and diversity.

What does it mean to be an entrepreneur in Oceania? This question needs to be answered as there is still uncertainty about what distinguishes an entrepreneur in Oceania from other places. Oceania entrepreneurship is not currently fully explained in the broader entrepreneurship discourse. This chapter will explore the role of entrepreneurship in Oceania by taking readers on a fascinating journey through the literature. This provides insights into the concepts of Oceania and entrepreneurship thereby offering compelling justification for more focus to be placed on Oceania in entrepreneurship research. The chapter contributes to the literature on Oceania entrepreneurship by drawing on existing works and practice. The strength of this chapter is that it adds a valuable contribution to the broader entrepreneurship debate about the importance of context. Thereby, this chapter presents important theoretical, practical and policy implications on Oceania entrepreneurship.

Oceania Entrepreneurship

Entrepreneurship is a contested topic due to the different definitions existing in the literature (Apostolopoulos et al., 2021). Most definitions of entrepreneurship refer to in general terms involving any kind of activity that makes a difference in the marketplace. This means entrepreneurs act as change-makers in society. The emphasis in entrepreneurship is recognising opportunities. Thus, in this chapter, a more inclusive definition of entrepreneurship is adopted. This means entrepreneurship is defined as any kind of innovative, risk-taking and proactive activity in a business context. Thus, there is an emphasis on certain behaviours that are evident in entrepreneurs.

Entrepreneurs do not have to be lone heroes or superstars but can also be ordinary people pursuing a business opportunity. Many studies suggest or imply that entrepreneurship requires ambitious individuals to pursue rapid growth. The odds of this happening are low as most entrepreneurship occurs in an incremental way (Ferreira et al., 2018). Thus, entrepreneurs normally create short-lived ventures that only operate for a short time period. The entrepreneur's original intention might have been to create a long-lasting venture but due to competitive forces, the venture lasts for a short time period. Entrepreneurs are less constrained in their routines and organisational structure. This means they can make quick decisions that enable them to pursue market trends. Therefore, entrepreneurs are more responsive to societal changes and efficient in developing business ventures.

The traditional entrepreneur takes risks for personal gain and is interested in financial outcomes (Apostolopoulos et al., 2020). In contrast, a social entrepreneur pursues social goals in the business pursuits. Thus, a social entrepreneur displays creativity but does so while pursuing social missions (Ratten, 2014). A social entrepreneur has a blended value philosophy that balances social and financial goals.

The field of entrepreneurship has made significant advancements with numerous theories proposed in the literature (Ferreira et al., 2017b).

Nevertheless, some fields of entrepreneurship are less represented than others in the mainstream entrepreneurship literature (Mota et al., 2019). Oceania entrepreneurship is one of these fields that still has yet to establish a large body of research. There are many reasons for this lack of research. One reason is the lack of general understanding about how to define Oceania or the reason for its importance.

While it is difficult to predict how future changes will affect the Oceania business environment, it would appear that further technological and societal change will increase the emphasis placed on entrepreneurship. For some time to come, entrepreneurship will be a key societal and public policy issue. Oceania entrepreneurship is a very dynamic field that will continue to grow. Research in new and emerging areas can inform policymakers and practitioners.

Oceania is a region of contrasts with areas of high technical capability but also areas of low economic development. There is ample evidence of entrepreneurship in Oceania from small-scale farms to high-tech windfarms. Thus, there is a vibrancy in the amount and intensity of entrepreneurial activity taking place in Oceania. Oceania entrepreneurship is sometimes poorly understood and under-represented in entrepreneurship research. This chapter opens a window into the changing nature of entrepreneurship in Oceania. Table 1.1 states the different environmental forces affecting entrepreneurship in Oceania in terms of the competitive, consumer and regulatory environment.

Table 1.1 Environmental forces influencing entrepreneurship in Oceania

Environmental forces	*Examples*
Competitive environment	Proliferation of small business Pressure to compete based on price Global economic growth and marketing
Consumer environment	Interest in new innovations Growing interest in social responsibility and the environment Focus on technological applications
Regulatory environment	Emphasis on start-ups Funding for research and development Interest in facilitating regional competitiveness

Future Research Directions

This chapter will demonstrate that Oceania entrepreneurship has much to contribute to research and practice. Focusing on Oceania is critically important in terms of understanding culture and societal factors. This means context is a key platform in moving the entrepreneurship research field forward. I believe that research on Oceania can help bridge the theory–practice gap. Accordingly, Oceania entrepreneurship research will continue to grow in the future thereby elevating the status of Oceania in entrepreneurship research. In the discussion below, I discussed several improvements needed in the field of Oceania entrepreneurship that will stimulate further advancements. These improvements I hope will materialise in the next decade as more interest in Oceania results in further research taking place. In order to progress these improvement ideas, actionable recommendations are suggested.

Entrepreneurial Attitudes

Firms today face intense competition due to the dynamic nature of the global environment and need to keep up to date with technological change. Developing an entrepreneurial mindset is needed in order to live up to market expectations. Despite more than a decade of discussion existing on Oceania entrepreneurship, its unique features remain misunderstood. This is perhaps due to the lack of understanding about the functional usages of entrepreneurship (Ratten, 2018). This has created confusion about exactly what is meant by the term Oceania entrepreneurship. Thus, more research is needed on different kinds of entrepreneurial attitudes in Oceania.

Entrepreneurship Outcomes

There is a strong bias towards stereotyping all forms of entrepreneurship in a country or region as being the same (Jones et al., 2018). This means that there is a general tendency to associate a specific form of entrepreneurship such as technology or sustainability with a regional context. Entrepreneurship differs in each country within a region. There are also local contexts that need to be taken into account specifically with regard to urban or rural locations. Consequently, findings that have been generated in a country setting may not be generalised to other contexts. This opens up promising avenues for future research that refines research perspectives. Research from other fields such as sociology and economic geography can inform Oceania's entrepreneurship research. This means that increased interaction with other fields is a promising area for future research.

Oceania entrepreneurship is a multilevel phenomenon as it can be analysed at the individual, firm, interorganisational and country level. At the individual level, more research is required on how family and socio-economic background influence entrepreneurial intentions. This link has been studied in much detail in the developed country context but further research is required on developing countries in Oceania. In addition, the role of education and government support on entrepreneurship in Oceania needs to be studied in more detail. This will help to understand how changing economic conditions can influence entrepreneurial behaviour. As there are a diversity of individual entrepreneurs in Oceania, more research is required on understanding successful entrepreneurs and the paths they have taken.

At the firm level, more research is required on how social networks have facilitated entrepreneurship. This includes focusing on the international linkages entrepreneurs utilise to grow their business. In addition, more emphasis is needed on how the diaspora in Oceania facilitates knowledge transfer. This can include understanding how immigrants have contributed to the growth of entrepreneurship. This would make important contributions to transnational entrepreneurship theory in terms of understanding how Oceania entrepreneurs can utilise their social networks in multiple countries.

At the interorganisational level, additional research is required on how partnerships are utilised to facilitate entrepreneurship in Oceania. This includes public/private partnerships that enable the development of entrepreneurial projects. It would also be useful to research more into how different industries such as health and education grow their businesses through collaboration. At the country level, each country in Oceania needs to be researched in more specific detail in terms of entrepreneurship policy. This means understanding whether there are any specific cultural factors that are more conducive to entrepreneurship.

Leader Influences

More information is required on how government leaders facilitate entrepreneurship in Oceania. This means determining what kind of policies are utilised to facilitate entrepreneurship. Research is needed on how different countries in Oceania utilise taxes and tariffs in order to facilitate entrepreneurship. This will help to understand the role of government policy but also firm-level entrepreneurship. Moreover, it would be interesting to research more into how culture influences intention to be an entrepreneur. This would allow more understanding about how social and historical factors influence entrepreneurship levels in Oceania countries.

Research Methodologies

To achieve a more comprehensive understanding of Oceania entrepreneurship, researchers must include new types of research methodologies. This includes experimentation and the use of real-time information to analyse responses to entrepreneurship. In addition, multi-method studies that include both qualitative and quantitative data should be used. This will enable researchers to obtain a better understanding about how entrepreneurship develops over time. The initial startup phase of a business might develop differently to the maturity or growth phase. Thus, researchers need to be cognisant about the impact of time on entrepreneurial behaviour.

Networking

Networking in the form of building relationships with others is a way of facilitating entrepreneurship (Ratten & Ferreira, 2017). Firms that collaborate with other firms are able to obtain knowledge that can help them pursue new market opportunities. Therefore, networking is contagious as it encourages more linkages to be formed. Networking does not only occur due to necessity in obtaining resources or help but also because of a need to acquire new information. This means more research from an Oceania perspective is required to understand how network ties exist in the business environment. Strong ties in the form of continual interaction can help in building trust amongst network members. Weak ties that are the result of infrequent communication can still be beneficial when specific types of knowledge are needed. Therefore, it is important to research the influence of both strong and weak tie network relationships. In addition, firms that develop their networks are likely to have more social capital. This can lead to an expanded support network that provides a valuable source of information. Thus, more research is required on how the intensity of network relationships can result in more entrepreneurial projects taking place. This can include more research on Oceania technical collaboration or R&D partnerships.

Performance Predictors

Performance management is defined as "a continuous process of identifying measuring and developing the performance of individuals and teams and aligning performance with the strategic goals of the organisation" (Aguinis & Pierce, 2008, p. 139). There is a science-practice gap in entrepreneurship research whereby certain geographic areas are being ignored by researchers. In order to improve the entrepreneurship research field, more research on performance in the region of Oceania is required. This will enhance our understanding of how entrepreneurship is conducted in Oceania and its usefulness to the broader literature on entrepreneurship. New scholarly knowledge in Oceania entrepreneurship is likely to be readily applicable to enterprises thereby helping to bridge the science-practice gap. Table 1.2 states the future research questions for each major topic regarding Oceania entrepreneurship.

Conclusion

In conclusion, this chapter suggests that we have just begun to scratch the surface of research on Oceania entrepreneurship. This means the linkages between Oceania and different types of entrepreneurship are just emerging. I hope that this chapter will serve as a theoretical basis for future work. This means the chapter will be a catalyst in encouraging others to research Oceania entrepreneurship. Therefore, I look forward to continued work in this field.

Table 1.2 Summary of suggested future research questions on Oceania entrepreneurship

Topic	*Suggested research questions*
Entrepreneurial attitudes	How are attitudes to entrepreneurship in Oceania different to other contexts? What is the relationship between country context and entrepreneurial climate? Is there a correlation between entrepreneurship education and entrepreneurial intention? How do government policies affect individual entrepreneurial attitudes? What kind of public policies influence entrepreneurial attitudes in Oceania?
Entrepreneurship outcomes	How does entrepreneurship affect other areas of society? How does entrepreneurship influence societal and cultural change? What is the role of entrepreneurial ecosystems in influencing entrepreneurship? What kind of rewards and incentives are used to encourage entrepreneurship?
Leader influences	How is entrepreneurship related to effective leadership? What is the role of leader's attitude and values in influencing entrepreneurial behaviour? What is the relationship between entrepreneurial leadership and performance?
Methodological issues	What is the appropriate level of analysis for measuring entrepreneurship? What individual level factors such as education influence entrepreneurship? How can firm-level entrepreneurship be measured at different time periods? How can broad and narrow definitions of entrepreneurship be measured?
Networking	How can social networks be used for entrepreneurship reasons? What kind of family networks are used in Oceania entrepreneurship? How are international networks useful in entrepreneurial projects?

(continued)

Table 1.2 (continued)

Topic	*Suggested research questions*
Performance predictors	What are the antecedents of successful entrepreneurship in Oceania? What are some of the factors that may predict performance of Oceania entrepreneurs? How is entrepreneurial performance measured in Oceania?

References

Aguinis, H., & Pierce, C. (2008). Enhancing the relevance of organizational behaviour by embracing performance measurement research. *Journal of Organizational Behaviour, 29*, 139–145.

Apostolopoulos, N., Ratten, V., Petropoulos, D., Liargovas, P., & Anastasopoulou, E. (2021). Agri-food sector and entrepreneurship during the COVID-19 crisis: A systematic literature review and research agenda. *Strategic Change, 30*(2), 159–167.

Apostolopoulos, N., Ratten, V., Stavroyiannis, S., Makris, I., Apostolopoulos, S., & Liargovas, P. (2020). Rural health enterprises in the EU context: A systematic literature review and research agenda. *Journal of Enterprising Communities: People and Places in the Global Economy, 14*(4), 563–582.

Ferreira, J. J., Fayolle, A., Ratten, V., & Raposo, M. (Eds.). (2018). *Entrepreneurial universities*. Edward Elgar Publishing.

Ferreira, J. J., Fernandes, C. I., & Ratten, V. (2017a). Entrepreneurship, innovation and competitiveness: What is the connection? *International Journal of Business and Globalisation, 18*(1), 73–95.

Ferreira, J. J., Ratten, V., & Dana, L. P. (2017b). Knowledge spillover-based strategic entrepreneurship. *International Entrepreneurship and Management Journal, 13*(1), 161–167.

Jones, P., Klapper, R., Ratten, V., & Fayolle, A. (2018). Emerging themes in entrepreneurial behaviours, identities and contexts. *The International Journal of Entrepreneurship and Innovation, 19*(4), 233–236.

Mota, A., Braga, V., & Ratten, V. (2019). Entrepreneurship motivation: Opportunity and necessity. In V. Ratten, P. Jones, V. Braga, & C. Marques (Eds.), *Sustainable entrepreneurship* (pp. 139–165). Contributions to Management Science. Springer,

Ratten, V. (2014). Future research directions for collective entrepreneurship in developing countries: A small and medium-sized enterprise perspective. *International Journal of Entrepreneurship and Small Business, 22*(2), 266–274.

Ratten, V. (2018). *Sport entrepreneurship: Developing and sustaining an entrepreneurial sports culture*. Springer.

Ratten, V., & Ferreira, J. J. (2017). Future research directions for cultural entrepreneurship and regional development. *International Journal of Entrepreneurship and Innovation Management, 21*(3), 163–169.

Ratten, V., & Jones, P. (2021). Entrepreneurship and management education: Exploring trends and gaps. *The International Journal of Management Education, 19*(1), 100431.

CHAPTER 2

The Job Satisfaction Trajectory During Entrepreneurship Entry and Beyond

Safiya Mukhtar Alshibani, Thierry Volery, and Ingebjorg Kristoffersen

Introduction

Life can only be understood backwards; but it must be lived forwards.
—Soren Kirkegaard

This paper uses unit record data from the Household, Income and Labour Dynamics in Australia (HILDA) Survey. The HILDA Project was initiated and is funded by the Australian Government Department of Social Services (DSS) and is managed by the Melbourne Institute of Applied Economic and Social Research (Melbourne Institute).

S. M. Alshibani (✉)
College of Business and Administration, Princess Nourah Bint Abdulrahman University, Riyadh, Saudi Arabia
e-mail: safiya.alshibani@research.uwa.edu.au

V. Ratten (ed.), *Oceania Entrepreneurship*,
https://doi.org/10.1007/978-981-16-7341-2_2

Career adaptability—how people maintain satisfaction, manage career-related tasks and transitions—has been a major interest in the vocational career literature over the past decade (Tolentino et al., 2014). The entrepreneurship literature is no different, as indicated by the recent surge of scholarly work about career adaptation among self-employees (Georgellis & Yusuf, 2016; Odermatt et al., 2017; van der Zwan et al., 2018). This rich literature shows that job satisfaction, seen as a measure of career adaptability, increases after entrepreneurship entry, but declines after a while. The boost in job satisfaction is temporary rather than permanent, which suggests that entrepreneurs experience ***hedonic adaptation*** to many aspects of their career (Hanglberger & Merz, 2015). In addition, an initial boost in job satisfaction can accompany large and persistent decreases in other domains of job satisfaction, such as leisure satisfaction (Odermatt et al., 2017; van der Zwan et al., 2018). Recognizing that entrepreneurs experience a honeymoon hangover period after entrepreneurship entry, scholars have suggested that self-employment is not a panacea for job satisfaction (Georgellis & Yusuf, 2016).

This study contributes to the body of research on entrepreneurship career adaptability, and specifically on the dynamics of job satisfaction. The aim of this study is to quantify the causal effect of entrepreneurship entry on various aspects of job satisfaction before, during, and after the transition into self-employment. We label these three stages anticipation, reaction, and adaptation periods. We expand the current body of research by taking a longitudinal perspective on career adaptability and providing a more granular approach on job satisfaction. Past research that draws on data from the Panel Study on Entrepreneurial Dynamics (PSED) has shown that entrepreneurship is a long-term process (Reynolds & Curtin, 2009). Therefore, it is essential to understand the evolution of job satisfaction before, during, and after the "official" entrepreneurship entry. In this study, we track the evolution of entrepreneurs' job satisfaction four years before they become self-employed, during the year of transition, and five years after the transition.

T. Volery
Zurich University of Applied Sciences—ZHAW, Winterthur, Switzerland

S. M. Alshibani · T. Volery · I. Kristoffersen
The University of Western Australia, Perth, Australia

We also provide a more granular perspective on job satisfaction, and answer Carter's call "to move away from the use of narrow and static measures and instead focus on a broad set of indicators that collectively contribute to overall job satisfaction" (Carter, 2011, p. 2). In addition, it is important that job satisfaction indicators capture specific aspects of the entrepreneurial career that require improvement (Georgellis & Yusuf, 2016; Odermatt et al., 2017; van der Zwan et al., 2018). This can be achieved by measuring within-individual variation of job satisfaction over time, especially during the transition into entrepreneurship and beyond. Many past studies have compared entrepreneurs with employees and, therefore, fail to capture the potential negative aspects of entrepreneurship (e.g., increased job insecurity and work pressure). By considering not only general job satisfaction, but other aspects, including job security, working hours, total pay, the work itself, and the flexibility to balance work and non-work commitments, we present a multi-faceted view of job satisfaction and the potential trade-off between the financial and psychological aspects of job satisfaction.

Drawing on the Household Income and Labour Dynamics in Australia (HILDA) survey, we examined the job satisfaction trajectory both before and after the transition into full-time entrepreneurship. We follow a similar approach to Georgellis and Yusuf (2016), but by considering an Australian dataset our research expands our understanding of entrepreneurs' job satisfaction in a different culture and institutional setting (Atalay et al., 2014). Moreover, we consider some important facets of job satisfaction that are not present in Georgellis and Yusuf's (2016) study, including the satisfaction of balancing work with non-work commitments and satisfaction with leisure time. These non-monetary rewards could be important mechanisms that assist to explain the adaption process in entrepreneurship (Georgellis et al., 2007).

The remainder of the paper is organized as follows. First, we provide a definition of job satisfaction in general and in the specific context of entrepreneurship. Second, we present a theoretical framework for the three stages of job satisfaction during the entrepreneurship process. We then provide give a detailed description of the data, measurement, and methodology used to conduct the study. Finally, in the discussion and conclusion, we give a brief summary of the results, a critique of the findings, and a series of practical recommendations.

Literature Review

The Different Facets of Job Satisfaction in Entrepreneurship

Job satisfaction is a central concept in psychology, occupational health, management, and economics (Boswell et al., 2009; Ulleberg & Rundmo, 1997). Overall job satisfaction has been an important predictor of many labor market behaviors, including productivity and performance (Kaplan et al., 2009), commitments and efforts (Boswell et al., 2009), mental and physical health (Dirlam & Zheng, 2017), and absenteeism (Ulleberg & Rundmo, 1997). Additionally, job satisfaction has been linked to general life satisfaction (Judge & Watanabe, 1993). Thus, indicating that people who have jobs that they like are more likely to have a happy life.

Job satisfaction is a complex construct and the most widely accepted definition was proposed by Locke (1969), who defined job satisfaction as "the pleasurable emotional state resulting from the appraisal of one's job as achieving or facilitating the achievement of one's job values" (Locke, 1969, p. 316). This definition espouses the view of a majority of scholars who consider that there are both cognitive and affective manifestations of job satisfaction. The cognitive component of job satisfaction relates to beliefs on whether the job is mentally demanding or rewarding. On the other hand, the affective component refers to job-related feelings such as anxiety, boredom, excitement, and acknowledgment (Aziri, 2011; Locke, 1969).

For entrepreneurs, job satisfaction is a measure of performance (Carree & Verheul, 2012) and it influences their future investment decisions, survivability, and persistence (Georgellis et al., 2007; Mattes, 2016). In addition, job satisfaction is a key contributor to a range of health and performance-related outcomes (Georgellis & Yusuf, 2016; Odermatt et al., 2017; van der Zwan et al., 2018).

Several studies have looked into the dynamics of job satisfaction and found that entrepreneurs are more satisfied with their career compared to paid employees (Andersson, 2008; Benz & Frey, 2004, 2008; Bradley & Roberts, 2004; Noorderhaven et al., 2004), despite the fact that entrepreneurs often have a lower and more volatile income, work long hours, and face higher uncertainty. Economists explain this premium by the *procedural utility* (Benz & Frey, 2004, 2008): entrepreneurs enjoy what they are doing rather than the final outcome. Another explanation is offered by psychologists, in that according to the tenet of self-determination theory, entrepreneurship as a career fulfils the basic psychological needs for autonomy, competence, and relatedness (Nikolaev et al., 2019). Therefore, these benefits of freedom, leadership, autonomy, and control all contribute to a higher sense of satisfaction.

Although past research has provided several useful insights, many studies have relied on cross-sectional samples that do not capture the dynamic change of job satisfaction during the entrepreneurship process. Understanding the temporal development in the job satisfaction trajectory as a life course perspective is important for two reasons. First, such longitudinal perspective is vital to theorize on career development. Second, the rewards from entrepreneurship are multi-faceted and differ in amounts and types through the different stages of the business life-cycle (Carter, 2011). As shown in Fig. 2.1, we consider three stages in the job satisfaction trajectory: anticipation, reaction, and adaptation. We posit that each stage has distinct characteristics.

The Anticipatory Stage

Anticipation refers to "all forward-looking attitudes and activities" (Oner & Tugcu, 2019, p. 111). It is about behavior that uses the future in its decisional process. The anticipatory stage can be described by a strong intention and emotion. In this stage of envisaging their entrepreneurship journey, individuals mark the entry into the new venture world by demonstrating a strong intention to start the business (Cheraghi et al., 2019). In the anticipation stage, would-be entrepreneurs start planning their business venture (Hatak & Snellman, 2017) and initiate a series of activities, including ideation, developing a business plan, researching the market, applying for financial funding, and building the supporting team.

Many scholars have considered intention as one of the critical elements in the entrepreneurial process (Iakovleva & Kolvereid, 2009). There is strong evidence that human behavior is planned rather than spontaneous when envisioning a new venture as a career choice (Krueger & Brazeal, 1994). This is because intention proceeds behavior and it provides useful insight into the process of opportunity recognition. The entrepreneurship literature is replete with empirical findings that intention is a strong predictor of new venture creation (Donaldson, 2019; Nabi et al., 2011).

Strong emotions are also a distinctive feature of the anticipation stage. Anticipated emotions have been deemed crucial when entrepreneurs evaluate a business opportunity (Delgado García et al., 2015; Foo et al., 2009). Entrepreneurship is conceptualized as an emotional journey (Baron, 2008; Cardon et al., 2012; Shepherd et al., 2015) and the entrepreneurship process starts from the entrepreneur's recognition, enactment, and regulation of positive and negative feelings (Riquelme, 2020). For example, Kato and Wiklund (2011), who analyzed entrepreneurs' diary blogs during the early stage of the venture, suggest that entrepreneurs were experiencing highly stimulated states in terms of both positive (i.e., hope, optimism) and negative effects (i.e., fear, worry, anxiety).

Similarly, feelings of dissatisfaction were also found to be a trigger into self-employment (Guerra & Patuelli, 2016; Nikolaev et al., 2019). For example, Kautonen and Palmroos (2010) found a significantly higher level of job satisfaction among nascent entrepreneurs and attribute this to the fact that nascent entrepreneurs are drawn into entrepreneurship because of low job satisfaction in paid employment.

The Reaction Stage

The reaction stage is the effective move from a latent entrepreneur to a nascent entrepreneur. This stage heavily depends on the gap between the entrepreneur's expectation of entrepreneurship and the reality that unfolds. These expectations vary from personal to business-related expectations (Hanage et al., 2016; Nheta et al., 2020). For many aspiring entrepreneurs, the reality of operating a business does not meet their initial expectations. Due to the complexity and dynamism that characterizes the entrepreneurship context, a variety of issues could arise. For example, as shown in Fig. 2.1, a latent entrepreneur may expect an easy transition but, more often than not, launching a start-up is a daunting process with many twists and turns.

High expectations about the new business can create significant stress and dissatisfaction when they do not match up to the realities of entrepreneurship. Expectations-reality gap theory suggests that the level of job satisfaction is determined by the gap between a set of expectations before the event and the realities that occur after the event (Michalos, 1985). As Georgellis and Yusuf (2016) remarked "expectations do not always materialize during self-employment, the expectations-reality gap widens, which has a detrimental effect on job satisfaction" (Georgellis & Yusuf, 2016, p. 54). In fact, up to sixty percent of new start-ups and new ventures failure within the first five years (Nheta et al., 2020). This high rate of failure may increase the feelings of job dissatisfaction and insecurity (Nheta et al., 2020).

The Adaptation Stage

The adaptation stage encompasses habituation and adjustment to the new career role (Gajda, 2015, 2019). Career adaptability, according to vocational research, refers to the capacity of normalizing challenging demands of a new role and is a key for career success. Specifically, career adaptability constitutes a "self-regulatory, transactional, and malleable competency that enables workers to successfully solve unfamiliar, complex, and ill-defined problems throughout their careers" (Rudolph et al., 2017, p. 17). In this vein, we define adaptation as a dynamic and multi-dimensional process through which entrepreneurs meet the new career challenges and unfamiliar tasks of self-employment. The result of the adaptation process is harmonious relations between the entrepreneurs and the new conditions of professional activity. That is, an entrepreneur reaches the proper level of professional success, revealing professional potential and preserving satisfaction.

In the context of entrepreneurship entry, the adaptation stage represents a gradual transition from the perception of being a paid employee toward being self-employed, while assimilating this new career as part of one's personal identity. During this stage, entrepreneurs have to adjust and cope with new demands, negative emotions, and occupational loneliness (Fernet et al., 2016). Past research has found that entrepreneurs tend to experience hedonic adaptation, so that their job satisfaction returns to the pre-entry level, or close to it in the case of partial adaptation. A high level of dissatisfaction has a negative influence on the well-being of entrepreneurs and can potentially lead to an exit of the career (Doern & Goss, 2014). Thus, hedonic adaptive processes are less desirable for entrepreneurs because they bereave them from the possibility of permanent joy (Doern & Goss, 2014; Oner & Tugcu, 2019). The prospect for a long-term career in entrepreneurship is therefore better for those entrepreneurs with greater career adaptability, rather than hedonic adaptation.

One of the major theories that explains hedonic adaptation is the set-point theory (Clark et al., 2008; Rudolf & Kang, 2015). Set-point theory states that people are fixed to a steady level of satisfaction and that they adapt to major life events, both positive and negative, then return to their stable levels of satisfaction. The return to this stable level, which is shaped by genetics and personality, is known as *hedonic adaptation* (Lyubomirsky, 2012). A major event will provoke certain behavioral and physiological responses to the event that eventually force the individual to go back to his/her set point (Luhmann & Intelisano, 2018). Put into an entrepreneurial context, the effects of the events related to career changes are usually transitory.

When it comes to self-employment adaptation, it is imperative to consider the different facets of job satisfaction separately, suggests several recent studies (Georgellis & Yusuf, 2016; Odermatt et al., 2017; van der Zwan et al., 2018). Entrepreneurship is about the balance between the financial, psychic, and social risks, and the rewards of a career in entrepreneurship that encompass both monetary and personal satisfaction. Job satisfaction in entrepreneurship should therefore represent the utility that the self-employed receive from the sum of all aspects of their job. We elaborate on these aspects in more detail in the following sections.

Job security is one of the most important pillars on which a person builds a sense of job satisfaction (for a review, see Hur, 2019). It is recognized that job security for an entrepreneur may be difficult with rapid and unexpected changes in the business market (Taylor, 2004). Additionally, the self-employed do not receive pensions, sick pay, paid holidays, and other benefits (Schonfeld & Mazzola, 2015). Furthermore, a large proportion of the difference in self-reported well-being appears to be explained by differences in satisfaction with job security suggests Dawson and colleagues (2017).

Satisfaction with pay is another facet of job satisfaction that needs to be considered. The instability, intermittent, and seasonality of income during start-up have been explored in relation to entrepreneurs' well-being (de Meza et al., 2019). The responsibility to get a return on investments for investors, who often include family and friends, tends to reduce the take-home pay for entrepreneurs and lead to additional stress (de Meza et al., 2019). These financial obligations may lead to dissatisfaction and make it difficult to return to the same level of satisfaction or even ascend to an acceptable level. It is expected that Australian entrepreneurs do not adapt to the same level of income in the entrepreneurial career.

A third dimension is the satisfaction with the work itself, which corresponds to the cognitive challenges of the work (Ford & Borgatta, 1970). The job characteristics of a career in entrepreneurship (i.e., utilization of ability, creative freedom, variety of job tasks, and intellectual stimulation) increase the sense of job enrichment, which in turn translates to higher satisfaction and a less adaptive mode. Past research has shown that passionate entrepreneurs persist, survive, and maintain their happiness (Marshall et al., 2018).

A fourth facet of job satisfaction concerns working hours, a prominent feature of self-employment (Cope, 2009). Entrepreneurs tend to work six hours more per week, compared to paid employees, which corresponds to almost an extra day away from their social life and leisure (Mcdowell et al., 2019). They generally have more control in arranging their work environments, work schedules, and workloads; yet, it may be difficult for a nascent entrepreneur (especially those coming from a stable "nine to five" paid employment) to adapt to longer working hours.

A last salient facet of job satisfaction concerns balancing work and family commitments (Mcdowell et al., 2019; Schjoedt, 2013). Entrepreneurs enjoy flexible scheduling arrangements, the independence of setting work hours, and the ability to fit their work around other personal commitments. Yet, they struggle with work-family balance especially during the start-up stage, which requires great time and effort to build a customer base, and a reputation (Padovez-Cualheta et al., 2019). Most studies suggest that this "juggling act" (Cope, 2009) has a direct impact on the ability to move forward with their entrepreneurial venture (Hsu et al., 2016). The high level of job satisfaction felt by entrepreneurs often comes at the expense of feelings of dissatisfaction with the limited time remaining that is available for other interests, including time spent family and friends (Binder & Coad, 2013, 2016; Padovez-Cualheta et al., 2019; van der Zwan et al., 2018).

Methodology

Data and Sample

The data for this research came from 16 waves of the Household, Income and Labour Dynamics in Australia (HILDA) survey. HILDA is a national representative data survey started in 2001 and sponsored by the Australian government (for full information about HILDA, refer to Watson & Wooden, 2002). HILDA's longitudinal nature provides an excellent avenue to test dynamic changes in job satisfaction upon the entry into self-employment and to detect the anticipation and adaptation effects.

In this study, entrepreneurship is defined in terms of self-employment. This variable is a self-reported information on employment status, thus the terms "entrepreneurs" and "self-employed" are used interchangeably. Our definition of self-employees follows Watson and Wooden (2002) and includes all types of entrepreneurs regardless of if they had incorporated their business or not. In other words, both owner-managers who operate their own incorporated businesses (treated in HILDA as "employees of their own business") and people who operate their own unincorporated business (treated in HILDA as "own account workers") were included in the study. Further, we defined entrepreneurial transition as the change in the occupational status from one year to the next, i.e., change from paid employment in year (t) to being self-employed in year ($t + 1$). This identification approach is common in economics and entrepreneurship research (Binder & Coad, 2013, 2016; Padovez-Cualheta et al., 2019; van der Zwan et al., 2018).

The sample was restricted to include only individuals aged 16–64 years, that were active in the labor market at the time of the survey. Further, we restricted the sample to the first time an individual made the transition into entrepreneurship (e.g., ignoring cases where multiple transitions occurred over the 16 waves). This procedure yielded 60,058 person-year observations of which 2152 individuals made the entry to self-employment (for the identified sample over time refer to Table 2.1). The reader should note that the sample covers the 2008 Global Financial Crisis year; that might have affected the investigated phenomena, which is acknowledged and addressed in the empirical work.

Measurement

Job satisfaction is assessed in HILDA by asking individuals to state their job satisfaction on a scale from 0 (totally dissatisfied) to 10 (totally satisfied). Furthermore, self-employed individuals were asked to rate their satisfaction level in terms of job subdomain, including job security, working hours, total pay, the work itself, and the flexibility to balance work and non-work commitments. These measures are frequently used in empirical research and they capture different aspects of the job, namely the subjective (or self-assessed) satisfaction (Binder & Coad, 2013, 2016; Padovez-Cualheta et al., 2019; van der Zwan et al., 2018).

Control Variables

Several variables that are potential determinants of job satisfaction have been included in the regression to fully capture the effect of entrepreneurship entry on job satisfaction. Specifically, we controlled for age and age squared; tenure (measured in years); long-term health conditions (a zero/one dummy indicator); education level (a set of three dummy indicators for having completed year 12 of high school, a trade qualification, and a tertiary degree; the reference group is year 11 of high school or less); home ownership; marital status (two dummy indicators for being married or de facto relationship, and for being widowed, separated, or divorced; the reference group is being never married); number of children; and income (log transformed and adjusted for inflation).

There is evidence that major life events have a direct effect on job satisfaction (Georgellis et al., 2012). For example, Georgellis and colleagues (2012) found that first-time marriage and having the first child has a dynamic effect on job satisfaction over time. Therefore, several major life events measured by several binary variables were included in the model, including: (1) pregnancy, (2) birth/adoption of a child, (3) death of a close friend, (4) death of close relative/family member, (5) death of spouse or child, (6) serious personal injury or illness of a close relative/family member, (7) serious personal injury/illness, (8) changed residence, (9) close family member detained in jail, (10) detained in jail, (11) victim of a property crime, (12) victim of physical violence, (13) being promoted at work.

Also, to control for general macro-level trends, year dummies from 2001 to 2016 and state fixed effects were added to the models. Furthermore, industry dummy variables at the two-digit Standard Industrial Classification (SIC) level were added to alleviate unobserved heterogeneity within industries (Toivanen et al., 2015) and to account for the proportion of the sample who changed their industry during the studied period.

Numerous studies have also documented the paradox of women tending to be more satisfied at work than men, with reasons including differential job values and motive (i.e., female entrepreneurs tend to be motivated by family commitments, and they favor flexibility in working hours); own gender roles and rules (Cheraghi et al., 2019; Sappleton & Lourenço, 2016); and sample selection bias (König & Cesinger, 2015). Consequently, given the focus of the study on job satisfaction and career dynamics, we conducted a separate gender analysis.

Analysis Approach

Following recent research in entrepreneurship (Clark et al., 2008; Georgellis & Yusuf, 2016; Hanglberger & Merz, 2015; var der Zwan et al., 2018) we examined the evolution of multiple facets of job satisfaction four years before switching to self-employment and up to five years later. This period of time measures the changes in the anticipation, reaction to the transition, and adaptation stages, providing a life course perspective. The approach recognizes that these different stages are marked by different aspirations, concerns, and commitments. Several dummies were created to capture the years' lags and leads for each individual after they made the transition to entrepreneurship. The model to be estimated is represented by Eq. (2.1):

$$\begin{aligned} JSC_{it} = {} & \beta_1 \boldsymbol{X}_{it} + \beta_2(S - 4_{it}) + \beta_3(S - 3_{it}) + \beta_4(S - 2_{it}) \\ & + \beta_5(S - 1_{it}) + \beta_5(S0_{it}) + \beta_6(S + 1_{it}) + \beta_7(S + 2_{it}) \\ & + \beta_8(S + 3_{it}) + \beta_9(S + 4_{it}) + \beta_{10}(S + 5_{it}) + u_i + \varepsilon_{it} \qquad (2.1) \end{aligned}$$

Here, JSC_{it} represents the job satisfaction components of individual i at time t; $\boldsymbol{X}$ is a vector of characteristics known to influence the DV (i.e., the control variables). The variables $S - 4_{it}$, $S - 3_{it}$, $S - 2_{it}$, $S - 1_{it}$ are dummy indicators used to capture anticipation effects (i.e., years before entry); the variables $S0_{it}$ and $S{+}1_{it}$, are dummy indicators used to capture the reaction to the new career in entrepreneurship; while the variables $S{+}2_{it}$, $S{+}3_{it}$, $S{+}4_{it}$, $S{+}5_{it}$ are dummy indicators included to capture the adaptation effects (i.e., years since entry). For example, the lead dummy $(S - 1_{it})$ is identified by the individual currently in paid employment, whereas they will become self-employed in the following year. Similarly, the lag variable $(S{+}2_{it})$ for the prevalence of being self-employed for one to two years (1–2 years) is identified by the individual being currently self-employed, being self-employed the previous year, but being a paid employee two years ago, and so on for longer lags (2–3 years, 3–4 years, 4–5 or more years). The last category represents individuals self-employed for five or more years. The sample only included one self-employment spell per individual, in order to obtain a clean estimate of utility while in paid employment and for the advantage or disadvantage of entrepreneurship after the honeymoon period. The final two terms capture individual fixed effects (u_i) and random residual error (ε_{it}).

Fixed effect regression is employed in order to capture within-individual variation in satisfaction over the sampling period, and to avoid bias caused by time invariant omitted information (Wooldridge, 2010). Consequently, results are strongly reliable even if there exist unobserved characteristics of individuals (e.g., fixed capacity to develop coping strategies for rapid adaptation) (Georgellis & Yusuf, 2016; van der Zwan et al., 2018). The time frame (four years before entry and five years after entry) was considered sufficient to capture the three stages, as there is some ambiguity in the literature regarding time given to people to adapt to major life events (Uglanova & Staudinger, 2013).

Results

The data was first analysed descriptively, exploring differences in raw mean of the job satisfaction's measure for the sample as a whole (Table 2.1) and by gender separately (Table 2.2). Entrepreneurs report the lowest levels of satisfaction around both pre-transition and the transition year. Further, the distributions for men and women are distinct, with slightly more dispersion in the female distribution.

The estimated coefficients of the fixed effects regressions are shown in Table 2.3, and a visual representation giving the complete pattern of anticipation, reaction, and adaptation to each facet of job satisfaction is shown in Fig. 2.2. It is important to note that the coefficients of these regressions could be interpreted in two ways: either they represent the dynamic effect in reference to the baseline level of the individual (i.e., before and after the transition) or between entrepreneurs who persist and those who exit entrepreneurship (Georgellis & Yusuf, 2016). Since this study aimed at exploring the career dynamics of individuals who chose entrepreneurship as a career, we focused on the former interpretation (Table 2.4).

A leading effect on overall job satisfaction (Model 1) is evident with growing dissatisfaction in the anticipation period, and then a substantial increase in the subsequent period (i.e., initial euphoria). The estimated overall job satisfaction trajectory of Australian entrepreneurs resembles in many ways the classic "honeymoon-hangover" situation highlighted in previous studies (Georgellis & Yusuf, 2016; Odermatt et al., 2017; van der Zwan et al., 2018).

In Model 2, the downward trend over the anticipation and adaptation periods demonstrates the existence of a strong and long-lasting negative effect on satisfaction with job security. This suggests that entrepreneurs do not bounce back to their "set point" level of satisfaction in terms of satisfaction with job security (Georgellis & Yusuf, 2016). Likewise, the pattern of development in satisfaction with total pay (Model 3) and satisfaction with overall financial situation (Model 4) are similar, with a noticeably gradual decline in the anticipation period. While satisfaction with total pay almost flattens out after the first year, satisfaction with financial situation alternating slightly in the first three years of the new venture. This pattern represents the entrepreneurs' negative response to the volatile income from a career in self-employment (de Meza et al., 2019).

The results also show a significant lead effect in the satisfaction with the work itself (Table 2.5) during the anticipation period and then almost a positive slightly downward pattern in the adaptation period. This suggests that Australian entrepreneurs' increase in utility may only be transitory and potential utility gains evaporate over time (Mcdowell et al., 2019). In contrast, the developmental pattern of satisfaction with working hours (Model 6) in the adaptation period presents a negative downward trend.

The satisfaction with the ability to balance work and non-work commitments (Model 7) and the satisfaction with leisure time (Model 8) display a sharp peak in the reaction period around the transition into self-employment. This suggests that the effect is not permanent, but rather temporary; and in accordance with the past research, this indicates a hedonic adaptation to be "your own boss" when becoming an entrepreneur (van der Zwan et al., 2018).

As it can be seen in Fig. 2.3, during the anticipation period, the dynamic effect on overall job satisfaction is similar for male and female entrepreneurs. However, job satisfaction is considerably more positive for female entrepreneurs both in the reaction and in the adaptation period. Similarly, female entrepreneurs are more adaptive than men in terms of satisfaction with job security. Also, women are marginally more satisfied with the work itself compared to men. The results are in line with previous studies which demonstrate that female entrepreneurs are in general more satisfied with their jobs than males as they have lower initial expectations and place less emphasis on monetary rewards (Cheraghi et al., 2019; Sappleton & Lourenço, 2016). In terms of the other job satisfaction facets, we observe a similar developmental trajectory for both male and female entrepreneurs.

As already indicated in Sect. 3.1, our empirical sample covers the 2008 Global Financial Crisis (GFC). In order to account for this fact in our estimation, we first examined carefully the year dummies in the models for any unusual behavior of these coefficients, though no such effects were identified. Second, we split the sample to before and after 2008; comparing and contrasting the patterns between the two samples. The result is consistent, and the developmental trajectory between the two samples are very similar (results available upon request). A possible explanation might be the generous social safety net in Australia, and also the fact that the GFC only had a moderate effect on the Australian economy (Kennedy, 2009).

Discussion

In this research, we aimed to explore career adaptability by measuring the dynamic change in job satisfaction associated with the entry into entrepreneurship. We extend the body of research on career adaptability in entrepreneurship (Georgellis & Yusuf, 2016), and specifically on the dynamics of job satisfaction by comparing and contrasting changes in job satisfaction during anticipation, reaction, and adaptation stages of entrepreneurship entry. Our study thus provides a life course perspective of the career development of Australian entrepreneurs.

This research contributes to the paradigm challenging the conceptualizing of job satisfaction as a static phenomenon that can be captured using cross-sectional surveys (i.e. Georgellis & Yusuf, 2016; van der Zwan et al., 2018). We concur with Aldrich and Zimmer (1986) who remarked that "entrepreneurship is a process and must be viewed in dynamic terms, rather than in cross sectional snapshots" (Aldrich & Zimmer, 1986, p. 3). In addition, failing to consider a life course perspective leads to inaccurate estimation of the effects of self-employment on job satisfaction. Prior studies in entrepreneurship and job satisfaction neglected the fact that each stage in the career trajectory has its own characteristics that form the entrepreneurs' perception of job satisfaction. This is problematic as "there is much to be learned by conceiving of entrepreneurship not solely as a final destination, but as a step along a career trajectory" (Burton et al., 2016, p. 237). New venture formation is not instantaneous but rather the outcome of an entrepreneurial process in which different stages may have different aspects of venture formation over time (Burton et al., 2016; Martinez et al., 2011).

Our findings highlight different patterns in the changes of the various facets of job satisfaction. First, the anticipation period was accompanied by feelings of dissatisfaction on all dimensions of job satisfaction. Therefore, the deterioration of job satisfaction precedes—and potentially triggers—entry into self-employment. These findings are consistent with previous research in this field (Benz & Frey, 2004; Hanglberger & Merz, 2015). Second, in the reaction period, entrepreneurs initially experienced a significant improvement in overall job satisfaction, but the effect was temporary. Similarly, the satisfaction with working hours, the work itself, and job security were found to be short-lived. There was an initial spike in balancing work and non-work commitments and leisure satisfaction, and a drop when entrepreneurs experienced the hard reality of establishing a new business venture. Satisfaction with work itself showed a positive and significant improvement.

These findings follow the contemporary theorizing on expectations-reality gap (Georgellis & Yusuf, 2016; Nheta et al., 2020; Odermatt et al., 2017). When entrepreneurs' expectations clash with reality, they discover that their hopes for their venture were obviously too high. Indeed, many nascent entrepreneurs entertain rosy expectations about their business. Most of them hope that success will bring them the freedom to work on their own schedules, market recognition with a highly sought-after product, as well as a level of financial abundance that their previous jobs could not provide. More often than not, the reality is completely different: customers are skeptical about new products, profits are few and far between, and entrepreneurs work long hours, spending most of their time doing everything other than what is most fulfilling or inspiring. This discrepancy in perception between expectations and the hard reality of entrepreneurship translates into a short-term boost in job satisfaction, followed by a decrease once the reality becomes apparent.

Overall, we found that entrepreneurs are dissatisfied with their working hours, their pay, and their job security, but they are pleased with their job in general. These nuanced findings could be explained by the demands and rewards approach. The intrinsic, intangible job satisfaction elements (i.e., the autonomy, flexibility, and fulfilment that comes from making a difference) are more prevalent than the extrinsic tangible aspects such as money and the number of working hours. Entrepreneurial career rewards are thus not determined only by business rationality (Carter, 2011). Job satisfaction is multifaceted and the multidimensional nature of entrepreneurial career rewards highlights the interconnectedness of different systems wherein the career unfolds. The trade-off between the "penalties" and "premiums" also suggests that different weights are associated with the intrinsic value of work drivers which influence the progression of an entrepreneur's career.

Finally, in the adaptation period, the set-point theory fits the observed pattern to varying degrees. Our results suggest that Australian entrepreneurs did not fully adapt to their new situation, but that they were rather prone to dissatisfaction with several aspects of their work. Among the more negatively rated aspects we found were working hours, pay, and security. A possible explanation is that some negative features of an entrepreneurial career resist hedonic adaptation. Such findings suggest that the interplay between entrepreneurship and job satisfaction is not universal, but rather context-specific (Anderson & Jack, 2002; Wagner & Sternberg, 2004).

Differences in how local institutions and cultural factors invite and reward self-employment may explain why these dynamics may differ across contexts (Boudreaux & Nikolaev, 2018; Fritsch et al., 2021). For example, Fritsch et al. (2021) looked at subjective well-being measures and occupational status and found that, for entrepreneurs, a country with more favorable entrepreneurial institutions is more conducive to their well-being. These results were echoed by Pathak (2020) who found entrepreneurs in societies with higher levels of well-being would be more resourceful to positively evaluate the feasibility of engaging in the entrepreneurship process. These researches point out toward the importance of contextualizing the entrepreneurship-job satisfaction relationship, as differences in cultural environments play a role in shaping selection into entrepreneurship and potentially could explain their roles in the adaptation processes (Shepherd et al., 2018).

Conclusion and Recommendation

This paper evaluates the long-term dynamics of job satisfaction during the transition into self-employment. We shed some light on the career adaptability of entrepreneurs by conducting a longitudinal study of the job satisfaction evolutions in the anticipation, reaction, and adaptation stages of career development. Our findings suggest that low job satisfaction precedes, and potentially triggers, entry into self-employment during the anticipation stage. The entrepreneurs experience a boost in job satisfaction during the reaction stage which characterizes the effective transition into self-employment. However, this increase quickly disappears in the early years of the subsequent adaptation stage. Similarly, the satisfaction with working hours, the work itself, and job security were found to be short-lived.

A number of limitations of this study should be noted. First, given the exclusive reliance on self-report measures, the results must be interpreted with caution. It is possible that certain responders may have been more inclined to provide positive appraisals about their career aspects. Although fixed-effect panel model estimation controls for what is perhaps the most significant source of bias, through the ability to account for unobservable time-invariant individual differences such as personality, there remains the possibility of bias resulting from time-varying unobservable individual characteristics, non-random measurement issues, potential self-selection, and reverse causality (Shepherd et al., 2018).

Second, the available covariates and their operationalization were limited by the available data. For example, occupational self-efficacy, goal orientation, proactive personality, and career optimism could be further explored. Finally, this approach does not allow us to test the individual variation in job satisfaction development. A person-centric approach is warranted to detect the variability and heterogeneity between entrepreneurs (Ritter et al., 2016). Future research could take a phenomenological discursive approach (Berglund, 2015) to study how and under which conditions these entrepreneurs anticipate, react, and adapt to their entrepreneurial role.

Notwithstanding these limitations, the research findings lead to relevant practical recommendations for several stakeholders. For potential entrepreneurs, satisfaction is a major personal resource that can help them to cope with the stress and ups and downs of the entrepreneurship journey. We advise potential entrepreneurs to lower their anticipation and carefully identify and assess their own expectations. Avoiding the expectations vs. reality trap during the entrepreneurial journey will help them to manage their identity during these transitions and to enjoy greater personal and professional satisfaction.

For policymakers, an effective policy design that is targeted at different stages of the entrepreneurship journey is needed. This study indicated that entrepreneurs face the greatest risk of dissatisfaction with security, income, and leisure. To prevent or minimize dissatisfaction, it is therefore recommended to pay more attention to these measures in particular. This could be achieved by formally training these self-employees about role expectations (Hanage et al., 2016; König & Cesinger, 2015). This role preparation may equip entrepreneurs with useful skills to avoid burnout and dissatisfaction, which would otherwise threaten their business success. Human resource managers in corporations should be aware that low job satisfaction is a push factor into entrepreneurship; they could potentially retain talents by monitoring the trajectories of job satisfaction among their employees on a regular basis (Singh & Onahring, 2019).

Appendix

See Figs. 2.1, 2.2, 2.3 and Tables 2.1, 2.2, 2.3, 2.4, 2.5.

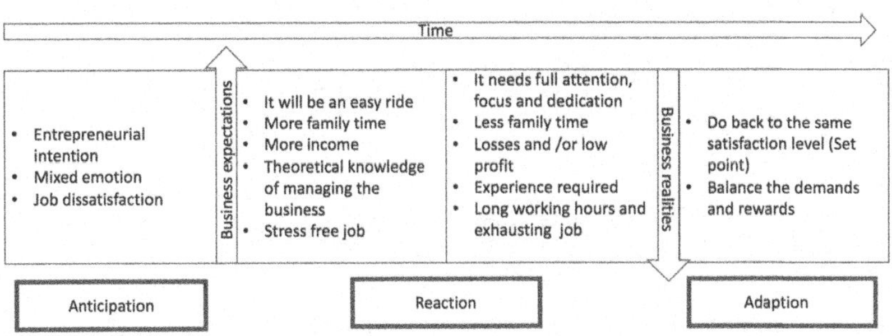

Fig. 2.1 Conceptual model (*Note* Adapted from Nheta et al., 2020)

Table 2.1 Lags and leads in raw mean satisfaction scores

	Number of obs		*Overall job satisfaction*	*Satisfaction with security*	*Satisfaction with pay*	*Satisfaction with financial situation*	*Satisfaction with work itself*	*Satisfaction with working hours*	*Balancing work and non-work commitments*	*Satisfaction with leisure time*
3–4 years before	858	Mean	7.55	7.86	6.76	6.32	7.62	7.04	7.47	5.89
		S.D	1.74	2.21	2.20	2.08	1.85	2.07	2.34	2.35
2–3 years before	1077	Mean	7.50	7.76	6.75	6.39	7.58	7.04	7.34	5.86
		S.D	1.71	2.24	2.20	2.10	1.87	2.17	2.42	2.40
1–2 years before	1394	Mean	7.47	7.75	6.74	6.45	7.59	7.02	7.42	5.93
		S.D	1.80	2.28	2.22	2.06	1.90	2.18	2.38	2.40
Within the next year	2152	Mean	7.22	7.63	6.77	6.33	7.33	7.00	7.35	5.86
		S.D	2.08	2.47	2.25	2.17	2.16	2.20	2.45	2.46
0–1 years after	2152	Mean	7.77	7.21	6.53	6.33	7.95	7.08	7.92	6.16
		S.D	1.69	2.52	2.42	2.22	1.78	2.19	2.22	2.50
1–2 years after	1120	Mean	7.67	7.54	6.54	6.49	7.92	6.89	7.79	6.01
		S.D	1.59	2.28	2.32	2.12	1.70	2.14	2.20	2.50
2–3 years after	901	Mean	7.80	7.44	6.69	6.52	7.96	7.12	7.82	6.02
		S.D	1.55	2.30	2.20	2.12	1.62	2.00	2.11	2.40

	Number of obs		*Overall job satisfaction*	*Satisfaction with security*	*Satisfaction with pay*	*Satisfaction with financial situation*	*Satisfaction with work itself*	*Satisfaction with working hours*	*Balancing work and non-work commitments*	*Satisfaction with leisure time*
3–4 years after	723	Mean	7.71	7.45	6.69	6.60	7.93	6.96	7.88	5.97
		S.D	1.50	2.35	2.23	2.11	1.57	1.98	2.03	2.42
4–5 years after	590	Mean	7.71	7.52	6.83	6.72	7.90	6.97	7.72	5.96
		S.D	1.54	2.20	2.26	2.00	1.60	1.92	2.09	2.30
5 or more years	485	Mean	7.82	7.69	6.93	6.74	7.97	7.11	7.91	6.16
		S.D	1.45	2.19	2.10	1.98	1.47	1.90	1.97	2.31

Table 2.2 Lags and leads in raw mean satisfaction scores by gender

	Number of obs			*Overall job satisfaction*		*Satisfaction with security*		*Satisfaction with pay*		*Satisfaction with financial situation*		*Satisfaction with work itself*		*Satisfaction with working hours*		*Balancing work and non-work commitments*		*Satisfaction with leisure time*	
	Male	*Female*		*Male*	*Female*	*Male*	*Female*	*Male*	*Female*	*Male*	*Female*	*Male*	*Female*	*Male*	*Female*	*Male*	*Female*	*Male*	*Female*
3–4 years hence	530	328	Mean	7.53	7.60	7.82	7.93	6.81	6.66	6.37	6.24	7.65	7.58	6.99	7.12	7.40	7.57	5.93	5.82
			S.D	1.73	1.75	2.20	2.23	2.13	2.31	2.06	2.12	1.80	1.95	2.04	2.12	2.28	2.44	2.32	2.41
2–3 years hence	665	412	Mean	7.51	7.48	7.74	7.81	6.74	6.78	6.39	6.38	7.61	7.52	6.99	7.12	7.30	7.40	5.92	5.75
			S.D	1.66	1.81	2.24	2.24	2.07	2.41	2.13	2.06	1.79	1.99	2.08	2.32	2.41	2.42	2.36	2.47
1–2 years hence	875	519	Mean	7.41	7.57	7.73	7.77	6.73	6.75	6.43	6.49	7.55	7.67	6.94	7.16	7.39	7.48	5.99	5.83
			S.D	1.77	1.84	2.27	2.31	2.21	2.24	2.02	2.13	1.85	2.00	2.09	2.33	2.33	2.47	2.36	2.48
Within the next year	1330	822	Mean	7.17	7.32	7.66	7.59	6.70	6.88	6.27	6.44	7.30	7.38	6.86	7.23	7.21	7.56	5.93	5.74
			S.D	2.07	2.09	2.42	2.57	2.23	2.27	2.18	2.14	2.15	2.18	2.19	2.19	2.45	2.44	2.41	2.53
0–1 years	1330	822	Mean	7.72	7.84	7.17	7.26	6.56	6.48	6.34	6.31	7.95	7.95	6.99	7.21	7.77	8.16	6.25	6.01
			S.D	1.66	1.72	2.51	2.54	2.32	2.56	2.18	2.29	1.69	1.91	2.13	2.27	2.23	2.17	2.41	2.63
1–2 years	732	388	Mean	7.56	7.86	7.53	7.56	6.55	6.52	6.45	6.56	7.85	8.04	6.80	7.05	7.69	7.97	6.07	5.91

	Number of obs			*Overall job satisfaction*		*Satisfaction with security*		*Satisfaction with pay*		*Satisfaction with financial situation*		*Satisfaction with work itself*		*Satisfaction with working hours*		*Balancing work and non-work commitments*		*Satisfaction with leisure time*	
	Male	*Female*		*Male*	*Female*	*Male*	*Female*	*Male*	*Female*	*Male*	*Female*	*Male*	*Female*	*Male*	*Female*	*Male*	*Female*	*Male*	*Female*
			S.D	1.57	1.61	2.24	2.35	2.26	2.45	2.07	2.20	1.69	1.71	2.02	2.35	2.21	2.17	2.47	2.57
2–3 years	573	328	Mean	7.68	8.01	7.34	7.61	6.67	6.73	6.51	6.53	7.93	8.02	6.97	7.39	7.60	8.20	5.94	6.15
			S.D	1.54	1.54	2.29	2.32	2.15	2.29	2.12	2.12	1.53	1.78	1.92	2.11	2.14	2.00	2.38	2.42
3–4 years	466	257	Mean	7.53	8.03	7.30	7.72	6.56	6.94	6.53	6.71	7.84	8.09	6.75	7.34	7.68	8.24	5.93	6.05
			S.D	1.54	1.38	2.37	2.29	2.21	2.26	2.09	2.14	1.52	1.64	1.99	1.90	2.10	1.85	2.36	2.53
4–5 years	379	211	Mean	7.51	8.08	7.42	7.70	6.70	7.08	6.69	6.78	7.75	8.17	6.78	7.32	7.43	8.24	5.82	6.20
			S.D	1.56	1.44	2.22	2.17	2.23	2.31	1.96	2.08	1.59	1.58	1.87	1.97	2.15	1.86	2.22	2.44
5 or more years	323	162	Mean	7.71	8.04	7.56	7.95	6.89	7.01	6.79	6.65	7.86	8.19	6.96	7.43	7.70	8.36	6.11	6.26
			S.D	1.46	1.42	2.22	2.10	2.11	2.08	1.99	1.94	1.45	1.48	1.87	1.92	1.98	1.87	2.18	2.56

Table 2.3 Fixed effect regression results

		Overall job satisfaction	*Satisfaction with security*	*Satisfaction with pay*	*Satisfaction with financial situation*	*Satisfaction with work Itself*	*Satisfaction with working hours*	*balancing work and non-work commitments*	*Satisfaction with leisure time*
		Model 1	*Model 2*	*Model 3*	*Model 4*	*Model 5*	*Model 6*	*Model 7*	*Model 8*
Anticipation	3–4 years before	0.002	0.166**	−0.011	−0.044	−0.016	−0.014	−0.067	−0.152**
		(0.055)	(0.069)	(0.068)	(0.058)	(0.060)	(0.069)	(0.074)	(0.072)
	2–3 years before	−0.093*	0.045	−0.042	−0.024	−0.088	−0.047	−0.186***	−0.160**
		(0.050)	(0.063)	(0.062)	(0.053)	(0.054)	(0.063)	(0.067)	(0.066)
	1–2 years before	−0.141***	−0.005	−0.102*	−0.026	−0.109**	−0.089	−0.176***	−0.090
		(0.045)	(0.056)	(0.055)	(0.047)	(0.048)	(0.056)	(0.060)	(0.059)
Reaction	Within the next year	−0.382***	−0.182***	−0.140***	−0.100**	−0.351***	−0.114**	−0.191***	−0.143***
		(0.038)	(0.048)	(0.047)	(0.040)	(0.041)	(0.048)	(0.051)	(0.050)
	0–1 years after	0.102***	−0.583***	−0.406***	−0.159***	0.235***	−0.094**	0.417***	0.167***
		(0.037)	(0.046)	(0.046)	(0.039)	(0.040)	(0.046)	(0.049)	(0.048)
Adaptation	1–2 years after	−0.019	−0.236***	−0.404***	−0.091*	0.149***	−0.263***	0.303***	0.014
		(0.048)	(0.061)	(0.060)	(0.051)	(0.052)	(0.061)	(0.065)	(0.063)
	2–3 years after	0.096*	−0.396***	−0.364***	−0.178***	0.217***	−0.116*	0.205***	−0.016
		(0.054)	(0.068)	(0.067)	(0.057)	(0.058)	(0.068)	(0.072)	(0.071)

	Overall job satisfaction	*Satisfaction with security*	*Satisfaction with pay*	*Satisfaction with financial situation*	*Satisfaction with work Itself*	*Satisfaction with working hours*	*balancing work and non-work commitments*	*Satisfaction with leisure time*
	Model 1	*Model 2*	*Model 3*	*Model 4*	*Model 5*	*Model 6*	*Model 7*	*Model 8*
3–4 years after	0.006	−0.364***	−0.381***	−0.162***	0.171***	−0.251***	0.337***	−0.031
	(0.059)	(0.074)	(0.073)	(0.062)	(0.064)	(0.074)	(0.079)	(0.077)
4–5 years after	0.020	−0.345***	−0.229***	−0.057	0.121*	−0.204**	0.216**	−0.069
	(0.065)	(0.081)	(0.080)	(0.068)	(0.070)	(0.081)	(0.086)	(0.085)
5 or more years	0.062	−0.301***	−0.301***	−0.135**	0.086	−0.052	0.437***	0.183***
	(0.050)	(0.063)	(0.062)	(0.053)	(0.054)	(0.063)	(0.067)	(0.065)
Constant	8.039***	7.789***	5.283***	4.232***	7.562***	7.308***	8.240***	7.004***
	(0.128)	(0.160)	(0.158)	(0.135)	(0.138)	(0.161)	(0.170)	(0.167)
Observations	115,816	115,679	115,702	115,837	115,822	115,811	115,750	115,817
R-squared	0.488	0.499	0.504	0.598	0.496	0.466	0.495	0.549
Control variables	yes	yes	yes	yes	yes	yes	yes	yes
Year Dummy	yes	yes	yes	yes	yes	yes	yes	yes

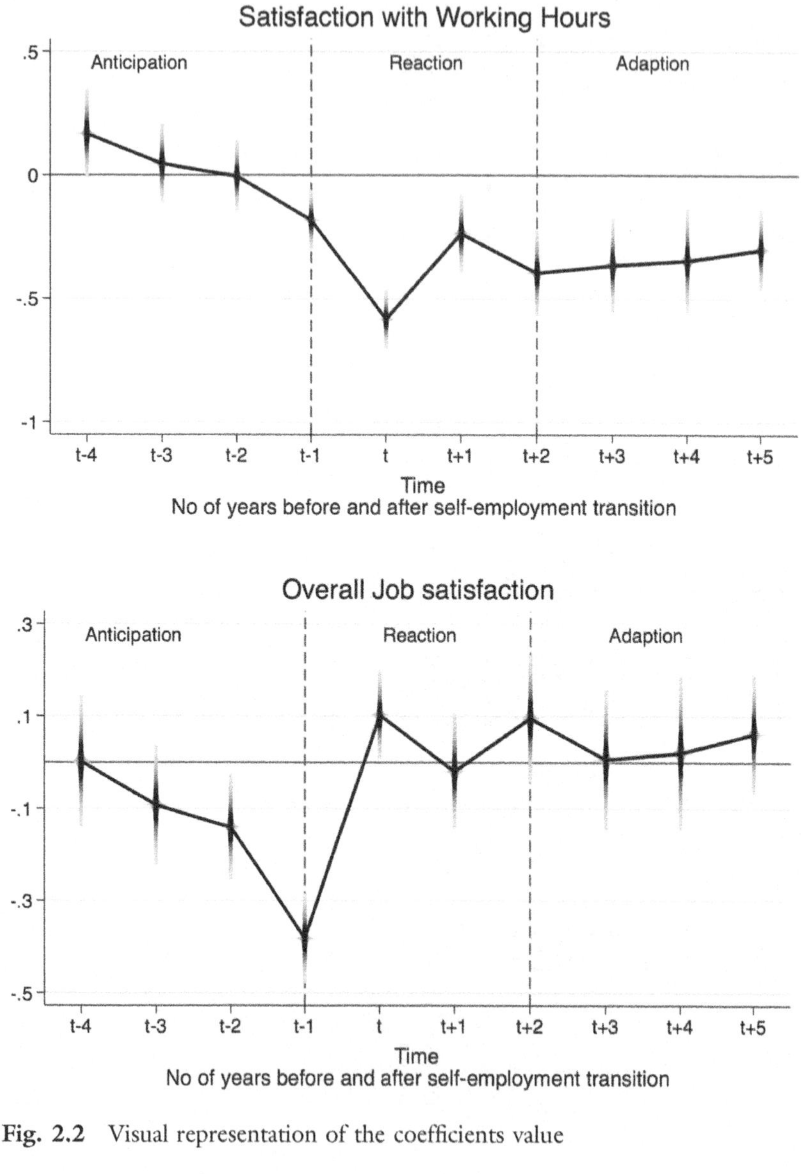

Fig. 2.2 Visual representation of the coefficients value

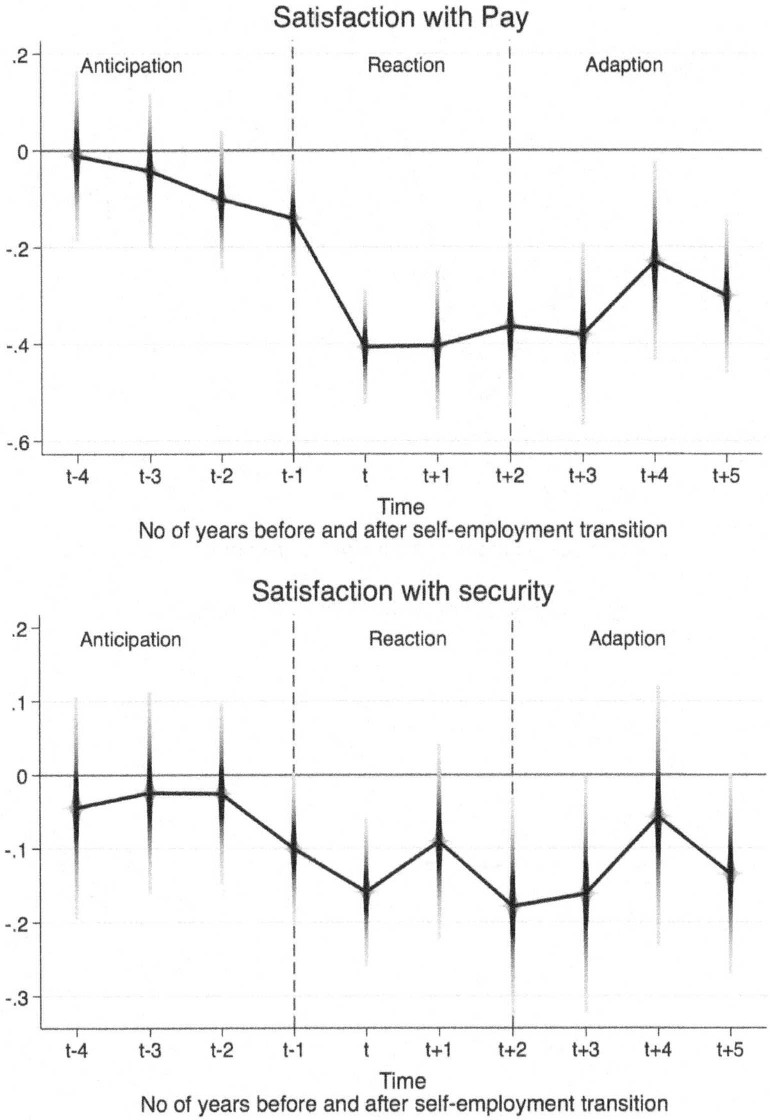

Fig. 2.2 (continued)

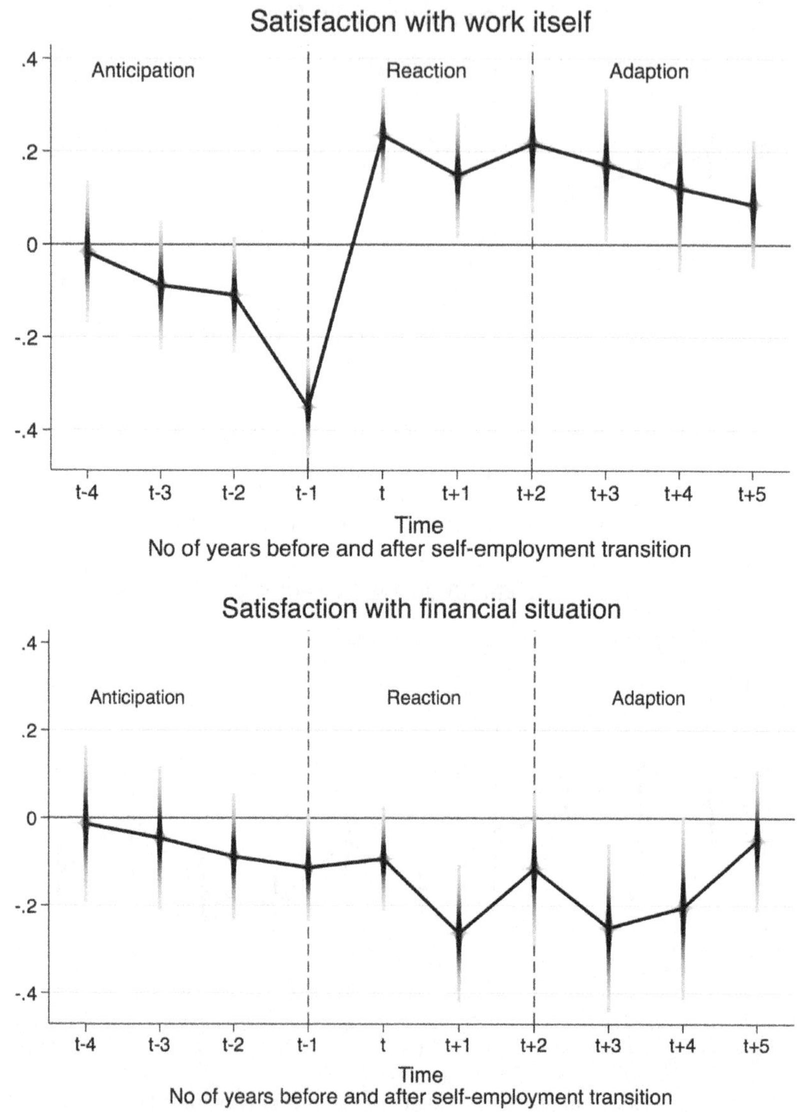

Fig. 2.2 (continued)

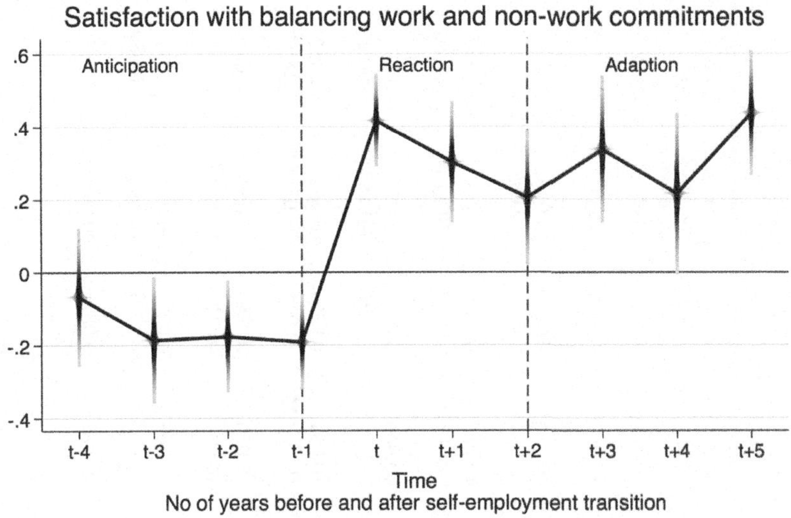

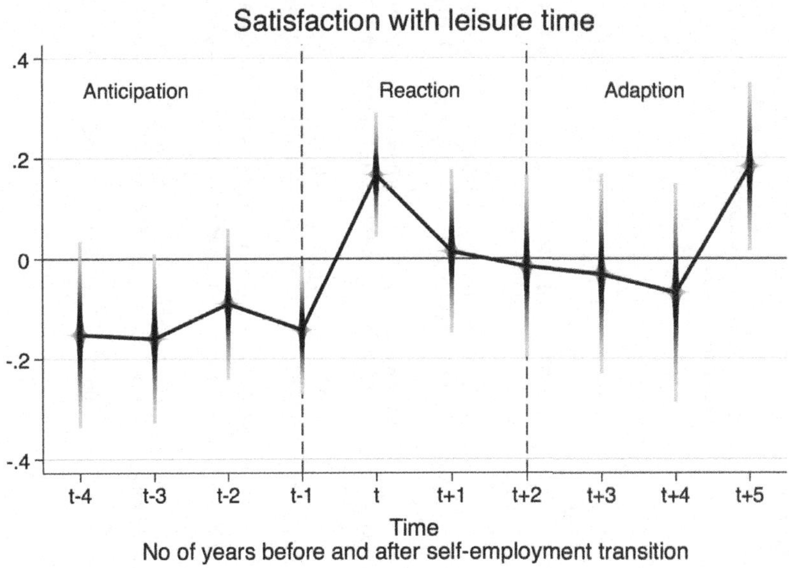

Fig. 2.2 (continued)

Table 2.4 Fixed effect regression results for the male sample

		Overall job satisfaction	*Satisfaction with security*	*Satisfaction with pay*	*Satisfaction with financial situation*	*Satisfaction with work Itself*	*Satisfaction with working hours*	*balancing work and non-work commitments*	*Satisfaction with leisure time*
		Model 1	*Model 2*	*Model 3*	*Model 4*	*Model 5*	*Model 6*	*Model 7*	*Model 8*
Anticipation	3–4 years before	0.079	0.133	0.110	0.036	0.005	0.069	−0.003	−0.123
		(0.069)	(0.087)	(0.086)	(0.074)	(0.074)	(0.086)	(0.093)	(0.090)
	2–3 years before	−0.022	0.064	−0.078	−0.043	−0.046	0.074	−0.087	−0.137*
		(0.063)	(0.080)	(0.078)	(0.067)	(0.067)	(0.078)	(0.085)	(0.082)
	1–2 years before	−0.147***	−0.032	−0.081	−0.015	−0.172***	−0.064	−0.113	−0.104
Reaction		(0.056)	(0.071)	(0.069)	(0.059)	(0.060)	(0.069)	(0.075)	(0.073)
	Within the next year	−0.355***	−0.147**	−0.174***	−0.173***	−0.351***	−0.096	−0.183***	−0.109*
		(0.048)	(0.060)	(0.059)	(0.051)	(0.051)	(0.059)	(0.064)	(0.062)
	0–1 years after	0.086*	−0.589***	−0.374***	−0.145***	0.215***	−0.066	0.405***	0.189***
Adaption		(0.047)	(0.059)	(0.057)	(0.049)	(0.050)	(0.058)	(0.062)	(0.060)
	1–2 years after	−0.034	−0.239***	−0.350***	−0.091	0.086	−0.224***	0.400***	0.081
		(0.059)	(0.075)	(0.073)	(0.063)	(0.063)	(0.073)	(0.079)	(0.077)
	2–3 years after	0.034	−0.457***	−0.359***	−0.135*	0.170**	−0.100	0.160*	−0.059
		(0.067)	(0.085)	(0.083)	(0.071)	(0.072)	(0.083)	(0.090)	(0.087)

	Overall job satisfaction	*Satisfaction with security*	*Satisfaction with pay*	*Satisfaction with financial situation*	*Satisfaction with work Itself*	*Satisfaction with working hours*	*balancing work and non-work commitments*	*Satisfaction with leisure time*
	Model 1	*Model 2*	*Model 3*	*Model 4*	*Model 5*	*Model 6*	*Model 7*	*Model 8*
3–4 years after	–0.075	–0.484***	–0.442***	–0.172**	0.105	–0.279***	0.324***	–0.001
	(0.072)	(0.092)	(0.089)	(0.077)	(0.077)	(0.090)	(0.097)	(0.094)
4–5 years after	–0.081	–0.333***	–0.326***	–0.067	0.054	–0.243**	0.074	–0.164
	(0.080)	(0.101)	(0.098)	(0.085)	(0.085)	(0.099)	(0.107)	(0.104)
5 or more years	0.057	–0.308***	–0.265***	–0.085	0.039	–0.054	0.401***	0.209***
	(0.060)	(0.075)	(0.074)	(0.063)	(0.064)	(0.074)	(0.080)	(0.078)
Constant	7.913***	7.669***	5.153***	4.218***	7.664***	6.993***	7.629***	7.197***
	(0.171)	(0.216)	(0.211)	(0.182)	(0.183)	(0.212)	(0.230)	(0.223)
Observations	59,072	58,994	59,033	59,080	59,073	59,071	59,030	59,070
R-squared	0.503	0.510	0.510	0.601	0.509	0.487	0.512	0.554
Control variables	yes	yes	yes	yes	yes	yes	yes	yes
Year Dummy	yes	yes	yes	yes	yes	yes	yes	yes

Table 2.5 Fixed effect regression results for the female sample

		Overall job satisfaction	*Satisfaction with security*	*Satisfaction with pay*	*Satisfaction with financial situation*	*Satisfaction with work Itself*	*Satisfaction with working hours*	*balancing work and non-work commitments*	*Satisfaction with leisure time*
		Model 1	*Model 2*	*Model 3*	*Model 4*	*Model 5*	*Model 6*	*Model 7*	*Model 8*
Anticipation	3–4 years before	−0.126	0.225**	−0.191*	−0.168*	−0.060	−0.142	−0.164	−0.192
		(0.090)	(0.112)	(0.112)	(0.095)	(0.099)	(0.115)	(0.119)	(0.118)
	2–3 years before	−0.214***	0.020	0.013	0.009	−0.171*	−0.238**	−0.350***	−0.186*
		(0.082)	(0.102)	(0.101)	(0.086)	(0.089)	(0.104)	(0.108)	(0.107)
	1–2 years before	−0.135*	0.037	−0.127	−0.034	−0.016	−0.132	−0.286***	−0.050
		(0.074)	(0.092)	(0.092)	(0.078)	(0.081)	(0.094)	(0.097)	(0.097)
Reaction	Within the next year	−0.426***	−0.229***	−0.096	0.012	−0.358***	−0.148*	−0.207**	−0.177**
		(0.062)	(0.077)	(0.077)	(0.065)	(0.068)	(0.079)	(0.082)	(0.081)
	0–1 years after	0.119**	−0.574***	−0.454***	−0.166***	0.251***	−0.145*	0.418***	0.147*
		(0.059)	(0.074)	(0.074)	(0.063)	(0.065)	(0.076)	(0.078)	(0.078)
Adaption	1–2 years after	0.005	−0.216**	−0.498***	−0.075	0.247***	−0.326***	0.125	−0.108
		(0.083)	(0.103)	(0.103)	(0.087)	(0.091)	(0.106)	(0.109)	(0.109)
	2–3 years after	0.193**	−0.297***	−0.361***	−0.235**	0.282***	−0.153	0.262**	0.061
		(0.089)	(0.111)	(0.111)	(0.094)	(0.097)	(0.113)	(0.118)	(0.117)
	3–4 years after	0.140	−0.151	−0.269**	−0.132	0.276**	−0.209	0.341***	−0.099

	Overall job satisfaction	*Satisfaction with security*	*Satisfaction with pay*	*Satisfaction with financial situation*	*Satisfaction with work Itself*	*Satisfaction with working hours*	*balancing work and non-work commitments*	*Satisfaction with leisure time*
	Model 1	*Model 2*	*Model 3*	*Model 4*	*Model 5*	*Model 6*	*Model 7*	*Model 8*
	(0.100)	(0.124)	(0.124)	(0.105)	(0.109)	(0.127)	(0.132)	(0.131)
4–5 years after	0.187*	−0.367***	−0.064	−0.028	0.226*	−0.147	0.441***	0.077
	(0.108)	(0.135)	(0.135)	(0.114)	(0.119)	(0.138)	(0.143)	(0.142)
5 or more years	0.046	−0.293***	−0.363***	−0.219**	0.163*	−0.073	0.470***	0.087
	(0.089)	(0.111)	(0.111)	(0.094)	(0.097)	(0.113)	(0.117)	(0.117)
Constant	8.179***	7.961***	5.358***	4.257***	7.416***	7.615***	8.935***	6.824***
	(0.193)	(0.241)	(0.241)	(0.204)	(0.212)	(0.247)	(0.256)	(0.254)
Observations	56,744	56,685	56,669	56,757	56,749	56,740	56,720	56,747
R-squared	0.473	0.487	0.500	0.596	0.485	0.445	0.479	0.547
Control variables	yes	yes	yes	yes	yes	yes	yes	yes
Year Dummy	yes	yes	yes	yes	yes	yes	yes	yes

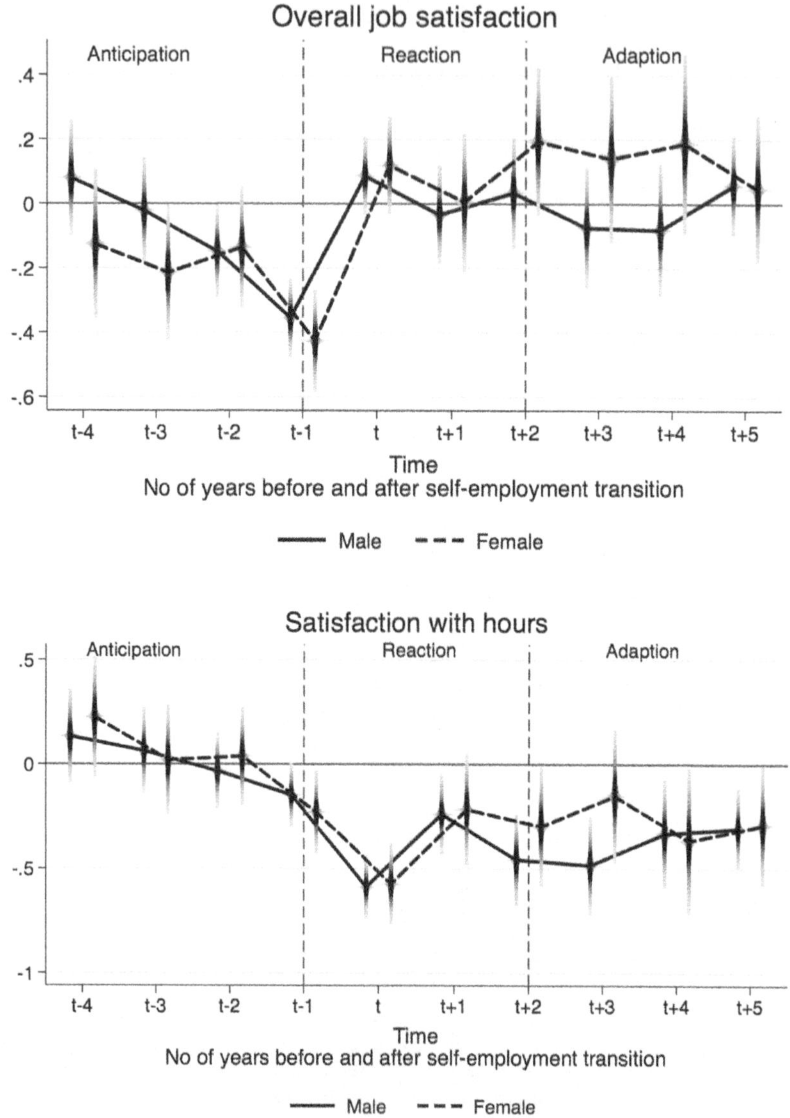

Fig. 2.3 Visual representation of the coefficients value

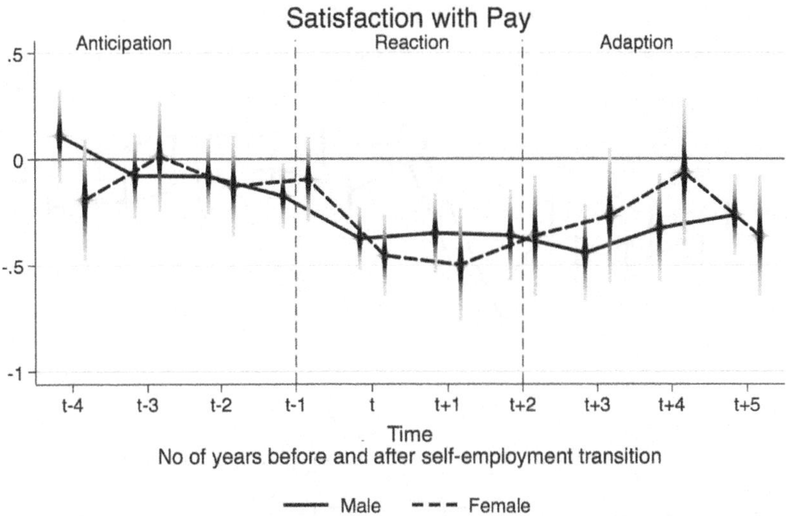

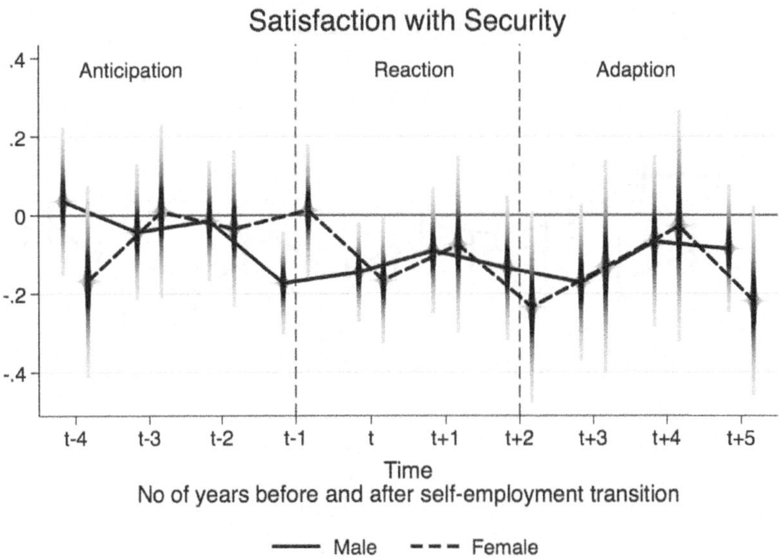

Fig. 2.3 (continued)

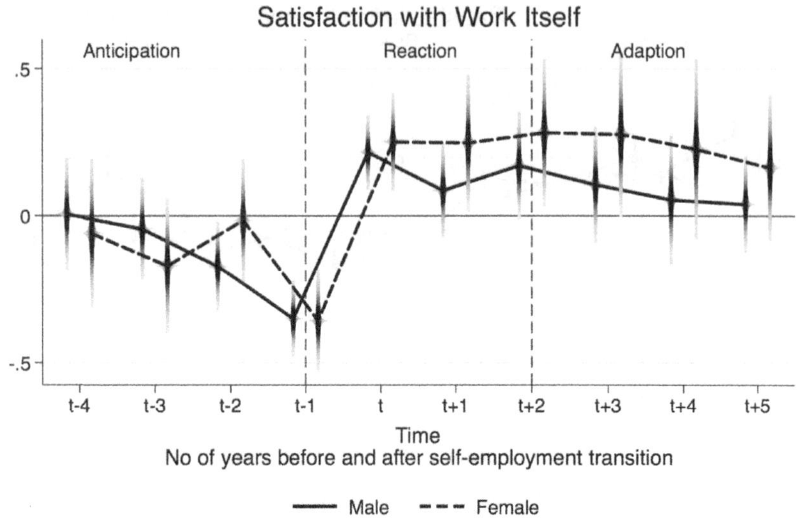

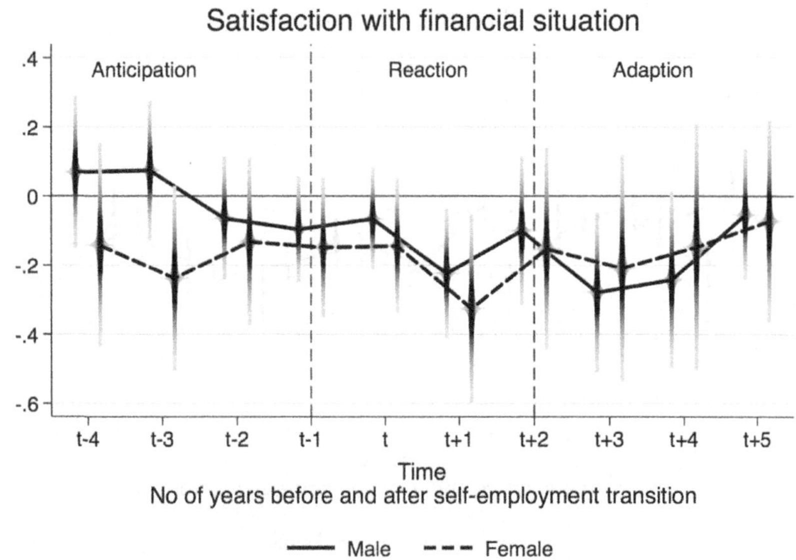

Fig. 2.3 (continued)

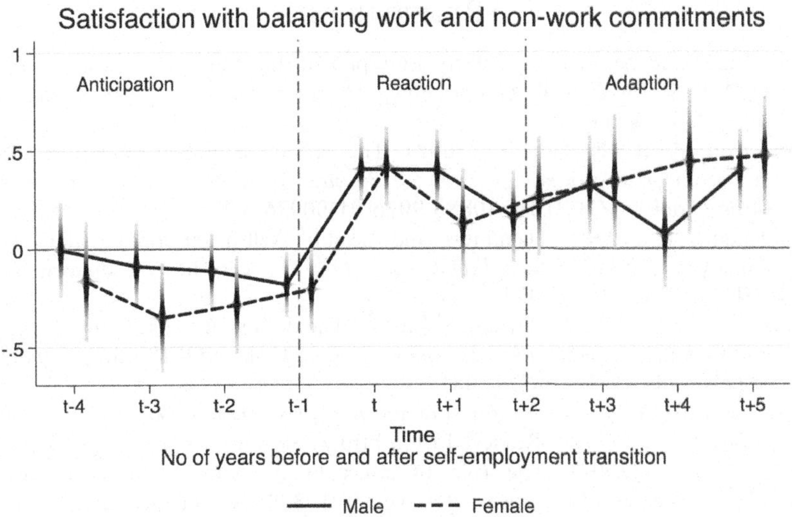

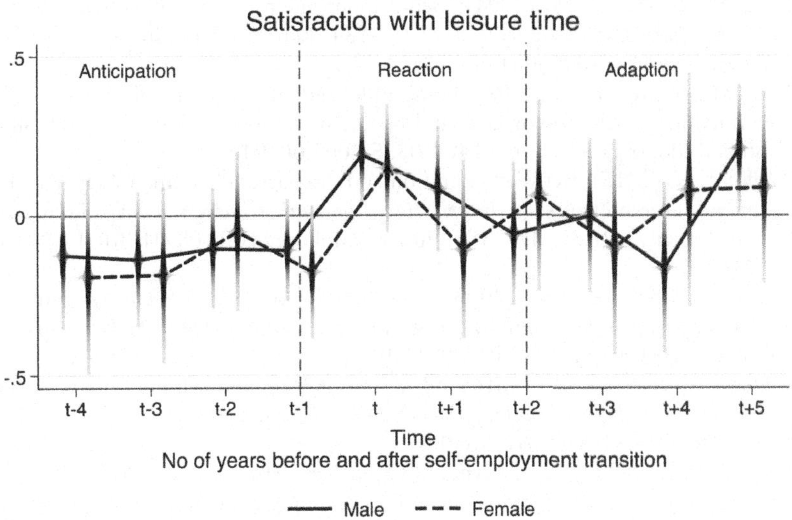

Fig. 2.3 (continued)

References

Aldrich, H., & Zimmer, C. (1986). Entrepreneurship through social networks. In D. L. Sexton & R. W. Smilor (Eds.), *The art and science of entrepreneurship* (pp. 3–23). Ballinger.

Anderson, A. R., & Jack, S. (2002). The effects of embeddedness on the entrepreneurial process. *Journal of Business Venturing, 17*(5), 467–487. https://doi.org/10.1016/S0883-9026(01)00076-3

Andersson, P. (2008). Happiness and health: Well-being among the self-employed. *Journal of Socio-Economics, 37*(1), 213–236. https://doi.org/10.1016/j.socec.2007.03.003

Atalay, K., Kim, W. Y., & Whelan, S. (2014). The decline of the self-employment rate in Australia. *Australian Economic Review, 47*(4), 472–489. https://doi.org/10.1111/1467-8462.12081

Aziri, B. (2011). Job satisfaction, a literature review. *Management Research and Practice, 3*(1), 77–90. Retrieved from http://www.mrp.ase.ro/no34/f7.pdf

Baron, R. A. (2008). The role of affect in the entrepreneurial process. *The Academy of Management Review, 33*(2), 328–340. https://doi.org/10.5465/AMR.2008.31193166

Benz, M., & Frey, B. S. (2004). Being independent raises happiness at work. *Swedish Economic Policy Review, 11*, 95–134. Retrieved from https://www.bsfrey.ch/articles/_409_2004.pdf

Benz, M., & Frey, B. S. (2008). Being independent is a great thing: Subjective evaluations of self-employment and hierarchy. *Economica, 75*(298), 362–383. https://doi.org/10.1111/j.1468-0335.2007.00594.x

Berglund, H. (2015). Between cognition and discourse: Phenomenology and the study of entrepreneurship. *International Journal of Entrepreneurial Behaviour and Research, 21*(3), 472–488. https://doi.org/10.1108/IJEBR-12-2013-0210

Binder, M., & Coad, A. (2013). Life satisfaction and self-employment: A matching approach. *Small Business Economics, 40*(4), 1009–1033. https://doi.org/10.1007/s11187-011-9413-9

Binder, M., & Coad, A. (2016). How satisfied are the self-employed? A life domain view. *Journal of Happiness Studies, 17*(4), 1409–1433. https://doi.org/10.1007/s10902-015-9650-8

Boswell, W. R., Shipp, A. J., Payne, S. C., & Culbertson, S. S. (2009). Changes in newcomer job satisfaction over time: Examining the pattern of honeymoons and hangovers. *Journal of Applied Psychology, 94*(4), 844–858. https://doi.org/10.1037/a0014975

Boudreaux, C. J., & Nikolaev, B. (2018). Capital is not enough: Opportunity entrepreneurship and formal institutions. *Small Business Economics*, 1–30.https://doi.org/10.1007/s11187-018-0068-7

Bradley, D. E., & Roberts, J. A. (2004). Self-employment and job satisfaction: Investigating the role of self-efficacy, depression, and seniority. *Journal of Small Business Management, 42*(1), 37–58. https://doi.org/10.1111/j.1540-627X.2004.00096.x

Burton, M. D., Sørensen, J. B., & Dobrev, S. D. (2016). A careers perspective on entrepreneurship. *Entrepreneurship: Theory and Practice, 40*(2), 237–247. https://doi.org/10.1111/etap.12230

Cardon, M. S., Foo, M. D., Shepherd, D., & Wiklund, J. (2012). Exploring the heart: Entrepreneurial emotion is a hot topic. *Entrepreneurship: Theory and Practice, 36*(1), 1–10. https://doi.org/10.1111/j.1540-6520.2011.00501.x

Carree, M. A., & Verheul, I. (2012). What makes entrepreneurs happy? Determinants of satisfaction among founders. *Journal of Happiness Studies, 13*(2), 371–387. https://doi.org/10.1007/s10902-011-9269-3

Carter, S. L. (2011). The rewards of entrepreneurship: Exploring the incomes, wealth, and economic well-being of entrepreneurial household. *Entrepreneurship Theory and Practice, 35*(1), 39–55. https://doi.org/10.1111/j.1540-6520.2010.00422.x

Cheraghi, M., Wickstrøm, K. A., & Klyver, K. (2019). Life-course and entry to entrepreneurship: Embedded in gender and gender-egalitarianism. *Entrepreneurship and Regional Development, 31*(3–4), 242–258. https://doi.org/10.1080/08985626.2018.1551791

Clark, A. E., Diener, E., Georgellis, Y., & Lucas, R. E. (2008). Lags and leads in life satisfaction: A test of the baseline hypothesis. *Economic Journal, 118*(529), 222–243. https://doi.org/10.1111/j.1468-0297.2008.02150.x

Cope, J. (2009). *The 'juggling act' of entrepreneurship: Developmental entrepreneurial learning and the concept of focal commitment* (Institute for Entrepreneurship and Enterprise Development Working Paper, 1–34). The Management School, Lancaster University. Retrieved from http://citeseerx.ist.psu.edu/viewdoc/download?doi=10.1.1.693.8179&rep=rep1&type=pdf

Dawson, C., Veliziotis, M., & Hopkins, B. (2017). Temporary employment, job satisfaction and subjective well-being. *Economic and Industrial Democracy, 38*(1), 69–98. https://doi.org/10.1177/0143831X14559781

de Meza, D., Dawson, C., Henley, A., & Arabsheibani, G. R. (2019). Curb your enthusiasm: Optimistic entrepreneurs earn less. *European Economic Review, 111*, 53–69. https://doi.org/10.1016/j.euroecorev.2018.08.007

Delgado García, J. B., De Quevedo Puente, E., & Blanco Mazagatos, V. (2015). How affect relates to entrepreneurship: A systematic review of the literature and research agenda. *International Journal of Management Reviews, 17*(2), 191–211. https://doi.org/10.1111/ijmr.12058

Dirlam, J., & Zheng, H. (2017). Job satisfaction developmental trajectories and health: A life course perspective. *Social Science and Medicine, 178*, 95–103. https://doi.org/10.1016/j.socscimed.2017.01.040

Doern, R., & Goss, D. (2014). The role of negative emotions in the social processes of entrepreneurship: Power rituals and shame-related appeasement behaviors. *Entrepreneurship: Theory and Practice, 38*(4), 863–890. https://doi.org/10.1111/etap.12026

Donaldson, C. (2019). Intentions resurrected: A systematic review of entrepreneurial intention research from 2014 to 2018 and future research agenda. *International Entrepreneurship and Management Journal, 5*, 953–975. https://doi.org/10.1007/s11365-019-00578-5

Fernet, C., Torrès, O., Austin, S., & St-Pierre, J. (2016). The psychological costs of owning and managing an SME: Linking job stressors, occupational loneliness, entrepreneurial orientation, and burnout. *Burnout Research, 3*(2), 45–53. https://doi.org/10.1016/j.burn.2016.03.002

Foo, M.-D., Uy, M. A., & Baron, R. A. (2009). How do feelings influence effort? An empirical study of entrepreneurs' affect and venture effort. *The Journal of Applied Psychology, 94*(4), 1086–1094. https://doi.org/10.1037/a0015599

Ford, R. N., & Borgatta, E. F. (1970). Satisfaction with the work itself. *Journal of Applied Psychology, 54*(2), 128–134. https://doi.org/10.1037/h0029050

Fritsch, M., Sorgner, A., & Wyrwich, M. (2021). Types of institutions and well-being of self-employed and paid employees in Europe. *Small Business Economics, 56*, 877–901. https://doi.org/10.1007/s11187-019-00274-2

Gajda, J. (2015). Social and professional adaptation of employees as a main factor in shaping working conditions. *Journal of US-China Public Administration, 12*(10), 789–795. https://doi.org/10.17265/1548-6591/2015.10.006

Gajda, J. (2019). Professional adaptation of new employees to the organization. *System Safety: Human—Technical Facility—Environment, 1*(1), 929–938. https://doi.org/10.2478/czoto-2019-0118

Georgellis, Y., Lange, T., & Tabvuma, V. (2012). The impact of life events on job satisfaction. *Journal of Vocational Behavior, 80*(2), 464–473. https://doi.org/10.1016/j.jvb.2011.12.005

Georgellis, Y., Sessions, J., & Tsitsianis, N. (2007). Pecuniary and non-pecuniary aspects of self-employment survival. *Quarterly Review of Economics and Finance, 47*(1), 94–112. https://doi.org/10.1016/j.qref.2006.03.002

Georgellis, Y., & Yusuf, A. (2016). Is becoming self-employed a panacea for job satisfaction? Longitudinal evidence from work to self-employment transitions. *Journal of Small Business Management, 54*, 53–76. https://doi.org/10.1111/jsbm.12292

Guerra, G., & Patuelli, R. (2016). The role of job satisfaction in transitions into self-employment. *Entrepreneurship: Theory and Practice, 40*(3), 543–571. https://doi.org/10.1111/etap.12133

Hanage, R., Scott, J. M., & Davies, M. A. P. (2016). From "great expectations" to "hard times": A longitudinal study of creative graduate new ventures.

International Journal of Entrepreneurial Behavior & Research, 22(1), 17–38. https://doi.org/10.1108/IJEBR-07-2014-0135

Hanglberger, D., & Merz, J. (2015). Does self-employment really raise job satisfaction? Adaptation and anticipation effects on self-employment and general job changes. *Journal of Labor Market Research, 48*, 287–303. https://doi.org/10.2139/ssrn.1884784

Hatak, I., & Snellman, K. (2017). The influence of anticipated regret on business start-up behaviour. *International Small Business Journal: Researching Entrepreneurship, 35*(3), 349–360. https://doi.org/10.1177/0266242616673421

Hsu, D. K., Wiklund, J., Anderson, S. E., & Coffey, B. S. (2016). Journal of Business Venturing Entrepreneurial exit intentions and the business-family interface. *Journal of Business Venturing, 31*(6), 613–627. https://doi.org/10.1016/j.jbusvent.2016.08.001

Hur, H. (2019). Job security matters: A systematic review and meta-analysis of the relationship between job security and work attitudes. *Journal of Management and Organization*, 1–31. https://doi.org/10.1017/jmo.2019.3

Iakovleva, T., & Kolvereid, L. (2009). An integrated model of entrepreneurial intentions. *International Journal of Business and Globalisation, 3*(1), 66–80. https://doi.org/10.1504/IJBG.2009.021632

Judge, T. A., & Watanabe, S. (1993). Another look at the job-life satisfaction relationship. *Academy of Management Proceedings, 1993*(1), 243–247. https://doi.org/10.5465/ambpp.1993.10317003

Kaplan, S., Bradley, J. C., Luchman, J. N., & Haynes, D. (2009). On the role of positive and negative affectivity in job performance: A meta-analytic investigation. *The Journal of Applied Psychology, 94*(1), 162–176. https://doi.org/10.1037/a0013115

Kato, S., & Wiklund, J. (2011). Doing good to feel good: A theory of entrepreneurial action based in hedonic psychology. *Frontiers of Entrepreneurship Research, 31*(4), 123–137. Retrieved from http://digitalknowledge.babson.edu/fer/vol31/iss4/1

Kautonen, T., & Palmroos, J. (2010). The impact of a necessity-based start-up on subsequent entrepreneurial satisfaction. *International Entrepreneurship and Management Journal, 6*(3), 285–300. https://doi.org/10.1007/s11365-008-0104-1

Kirkegaard, S. A. (1843). The Journals of Søren Kierkegaard. *Journal IV A 164.* Retrieved from http://sorenkierkegaard.org/kierkegaard-links.html

Kennedy, S. (2009). *Australia's response to the global financial crisis a speech to the Australia Israel leadership forum*. Retrieved from https://treasury.gov.au/sites/default/files/2019-03/Australia_Israel_Leadership_Forum.pdf

König, S., & Cesinger, B. (2015). Gendered work–family conflict in Germany: Do self-employment and flexibility matter? *Work, Employment and Society, 29*(4), 531–549. https://doi.org/10.1177/0950017014545264

Krueger, N. F., & Brazeal, D. V. (1994). Entrepreneurial potential and potential entrepreneurs. *Entrepreneurship: Theory and Practice, 18*(3), 91–104. https://doi.org/10.2139/ssrn.1505244

Locke, E. A. (1969). What is job satisfaction? *Organizational Behaviour and Human Performance, 336*, 309–336. https://doi.org/10.1016/0030-5073(69)90013-0

Luhmann, M., & Intelisano, S. (2018). Hedonic adaptation and the set point for subjective well-being. *Handbook of Well-Being*, 1–26. nobascholar.com

Lyubomirsky, S. (2012). Hedonic adaptation to positive and negative experiences. In S. Folkman (Ed.), *The Oxford handbook of stress, health, and coping* (pp. 200–224). Oxford University Press. https://doi.org/10.1093/oxfordhb/9780195375343.013.0011

Marshall, D. R., Dibrell, C., & Eddleston, K. A. (2018). What keeps them going? Socio-cognitive entrepreneurial career continuance. *Small Business Economics*, 1–16. https://doi.org/10.1007/s11187-018-0055-z

Martinez, M. A., Yang, T., & Aldrich, H. E. (2011). Entrepreneurship as an evolutionary process: Research progress and challenges. *Entrepreneurship Research Journal, 1*(1). https://doi.org/10.2202/2157-5665.1009

Mattes, J. (2016). The impact of transitions into wage-employment for satisfied and unsatisfied entrepreneurs: A Bayesian analysis. *International Journal of Entrepreneurial Behaviour and Research, 22*(3), 375–397. https://doi.org/10.1108/IJEBR-06-2015-0142

Mcdowell, W. C., Matthews, L. M., Matthews, R. L., Aaron, J. R., Edmondson, D. R., & Ward, C. B. (2019). The price of success: Balancing the effects of entrepreneurial commitment, work-family conflict and emotional exhaustion on job satisfaction. *International Entrepreneurship and Management Journal, 15*, 1179–1192. https://doi.org/10.1007/s11365-019-00581-w

Michalos, A. C. (1985). Multiple Discrepancies Theory (MDT). *Social Indicators Research, 16*(4), 347–413. https://doi.org/10.1007/BF00333288

Nabi, G., Liñán, F., Iakovleva, T., Kolvereid, L., & Stephan, U. (2011). Entrepreneurial intentions in developing and developed countries. *Education & Training, 53*(5), 353–370. https://doi.org/10.1108/00400911111147686

Nheta, D. S., Shambare, R., Sigauke, C., & Tshipala, N. (2020). Entrepreneurship gaps framework model: An early-stage business diagnostic tool. *The Southern African Journal of Entrepreneurship and Small Business Management, 12*(1), 1–7. https://doi.org/10.4102/sajesbm.v12i1.297

Nikolaev, B., Shir, N., & Wiklund, J. (2019). Dispositional positive and negative affect and self-employment transitions: The mediating role of job satisfaction.

Entrepreneurship: Theory and Practice, 44(3), 451–474. https://doi.org/10.1177/1042258718818357

Noorderhaven, N., Thurik, R., Wennekers, S., & van Ste, A. (2004). The role of dissatisfaction and per capita income in explaining self-employment across 15 European countries. *Entrepreneurship: Theory and Practice, 28*(5), 447–466. https://doi.org/10.1111/j.1540-6520.2004.00057.x

Odermatt, R., Powdthavee, N., & Stutzer, A. (2017). *Overoptimistic entrepreneurs: Predicting wellbeing consequences of overoptimistic entrepreneurs: Predicting wellbeing consequences of self-employment*. IZA Discussion Paper Series (11098). Retrieved from http://linkinghub.elsevier.com/retrieve/pii/S0165176599002426

Oner, M., & Tugcu, K., (2019). *Anticipation and entrepreneurship. In Anticipation: Conceptual, theoretical and empirical issues*. Yeditepe University Press. Retrieved from http://yuvam.yeditepe.edu.tr/pdf/Anticipation.pdf

Padovez-Cualheta, L., Borges, C., Camargo, A., & Tavares, L. (2019). An entrepreneurial career impacts on job and family satisfaction. *RAUSP Management Journal, 54*(2), 125–140. https://doi.org/10.1108/RAUSP-09-2018-0081

Pathak, S. (2020). Contextualizing well-being for entrepreneurship. *Business & Society*. https://doi.org/10.1177/0007650320927688

Reynolds, P. D., & Curtin, R. T. (Eds.). (2009). *New firm creation in the United States: Preliminary explorations with the PSED II data set (preliminary title)*. Springer.

Riquelme, H. E. (2020). Anticipated emotions and their effects on risk and opportunity evaluations. *Journal of International Entrepreneurship*. https://doi.org/10.1007/s10843-019-00262-3

Ritter, K. J., Matthews, R. A., Ford, M. T., & Henderson, A. A. (2016). Understanding role stressors and job satisfaction over time using adaptation theory. *Journal of Applied Psychology, 101*(12), 1655–1669. https://doi.org/10.1037/apl0000152

Rudolf, R., & Kang, S. J. (2015). Lags and leads in life satisfaction in Korea: When gender matters. *Feminist Economics, 21*(1), 136–163. https://doi.org/10.1080/13545701.2014.967708

Rudolph, C. W., Lavigne, K. N., & Zacher, H. (2017). Career adaptability: A meta-analysis of relationships with measures of adaptivity, adapting responses, and adaptation results. *Journal of Vocational Behavior, 98*, 17–34. https://doi.org/10.1016/j.jvb.2016.09.002

Sappleton, N., & Lourenço, F. (2016). Work satisfaction of the self-employed: The roles of work autonomy, working hours, gender and sector of self-employment. *International Journal of Entrepreneurship and Innovation, 17*(2), 89–99. https://doi.org/10.1177/1465750316648574

Schjoedt, L. (2013). The influence of work-and-family conflict on male entrepreneurs' life satisfaction: A comparison of entrepreneurs and non-entrepreneurs. *Journal of Small Business and Entrepreneurship, 26*(1), 45–65. https://doi.org/10.1080/08276331.2012.761802

Schonfeld, I. S., & Mazzola, J. J. (2015). A qualitative study of stress in individuals self-employed in solo businesses. *Journal of Occupational Health Psychology, 20*(4), 501–513. https://doi.org/10.1037/a0038804

Shepherd, D. A., Wennberg, K., Suddaby, R., & Wiklund, J. (2018). What are we explaining? A review and agenda on initiating, engaging, performing, and contextualizing entrepreneurship. *Journal of Management, 45*(1), 159–196. https://doi.org/10.1177/0149206318799443

Shepherd, D. A., Williams, T. A., & Patzelt, H. (2015). Thinking about entrepreneurial decision making: Review and research agenda. *Journal of Management, 41*(1), 11–46. https://doi.org/10.1177/0149206314541153

Singh, K. D., & Onahring, B. D. (2019). Entrepreneurial intention, job satisfaction and organisation commitment—Construct of a research model through literature review. *Journal of Global Entrepreneurship Research, 9*(1), 1–18. https://doi.org/10.1186/s40497-018-0134-2

Taylor, M. (2004). Self-employment in Britain: When, who and why? *Swedish Economic Policy Review, 11*(2004), 139–173. Retrieved from http://repository.essex.ac.uk/7894/

Toivanen, S., Mellner, C., & Vinberg, S. (2015). Self-employed persons in Sweden—Mortality differentials by industrial sector and enterprise legal form: A five-year follow-up study. *American Journal of Industrial Medicine, 58*(1), 21–32. https://doi.org/10.1002/ajim.22387

Tolentino, L. R., Garcia, M., Lu, V. N., Restubog, S. L. D., Bordia, P., & Plewa, C. (2014). Career adaptation: The relation of adaptability to goal orientation, proactive personality, and career optimism. *Journal of Vocational Behavior, 84*(1), 39–48. https://doi.org/10.1016/j.jvb.2013.11.004

Uglanova, E. A., & Staudinger, U. M. (2013). Zooming in on life events: Is hedonic adaptation sensitive to the temporal distance from the event? *Social Indicators Research, 111*(1), 265–286. https://doi.org/10.1007/s11205-012-0004-1

Ulleberg, P., & Rundmo, T. (1997). Job stress, social support, job satisfaction and absenteeism among offshore oil personnel. *Work and Stress, 11*(3), 215–228. https://doi.org/10.1080/02678379708256836

van der Zwan, P., Hessels, J., & Rietveld, C. A. (2018). Self-employment and satisfaction with life, work, and leisure. *Journal of Economic Psychology, 64*, 73–88. https://doi.org/10.1016/j.joep.2017.12.001

Wagner, J., & Sternberg, R. (2004). Start-up activities, individual characteristics, and the regional milieu: Lessons for entrepreneurship support policies from

German micro data. *Annals of Regional Science, 38*(2), 219–240. https://doi.org/10.1007/s00168-004-0193-x

Watson, N., & Wooden, M. (2002). The HILDA survey: What's in it for economists? *Australian Journal of Labour Economics, 5*(3), 397. Retrieved from https://search.informit.com.au/documentSummary;dn=147864980928106;res=IELBUS

Wooldridge, J. M. (2010). *Econometric analysis of cross section and panel data*. MIT Press.

CHAPTER 3

Coronavirus (COVID-19): Policy Responses for SMEs in Australia

Esha Thukral

Introduction

Coronavirus first emerged in Wuhan, China, and due to its subsequent spread, it became the health issue of the world. The virus in itself is extremely contagious, as it not only transmits rapidly but also continuously evolves. The earliest date of its symptom onset was 1 December 2019 (Liu et al., 2020). To contain and manage the spread of the virus, various countries placed restrictions on public events and gatherings thereby affecting the hospitality industry, travel tourism industry, food service, sports activities/events, causing a decrease in the overall economic activity. With reduced economic activity and lockdown, unemployment rates started to rise, causing a reduction in consumer spending and compounding the stress on economies and local businesses (Ratten,

E. Thukral (✉)
Department of Management, Sport and Tourism, La Trobe Business School, La Trobe University, Melbourne, VIC, Australia
e-mail: t.esha@latrobe.edu.au

V. Ratten (ed.), *Oceania Entrepreneurship*,
https://doi.org/10.1007/978-981-16-7341-2_3

2020). Thus, the pandemic, a health crisis, also triggered a major economic crisis.

Small and Medium Enterprises (SMEs) have been hardest hit by the Coronavirus, as sectors like retail, hospitality, entertainment, travel and tourism, and food services are overrepresented by SMEs. All around the world, SMEs are experiencing challenging times as they tend to have limited cash reserves and fewer assets when compared with larger enterprises (Albaz et al., 2020).

Australia is no exception when it comes to feeling the impact of Coronavirus. The first case of the novel Coronavirus was reported in Australia on 25 January 2020, a Chinese national who flew from Guangzhou to Melbourne. Eventually, on 23 March 2020, Australia announced the closure of all clubs, bars, restaurants, casinos, cinemas, gyms, and places of worship (Handley, 2020).

Along with the closure of non-essential businesses, the federal government also introduced social distancing practices. It got the businesses especially SMEs, in extreme distress as all these measures would invariably lead to job and income losses. In mid-March 2020, the Australian Bureau of Statistics highlighted that 86% of surveyed Australian businesses expected to be impacted by the COVID-19 in the coming months. However, the Government introduced a range of business support policy measures to keep the businesses in "hibernating" until the spread of the virus is contained and it's safe to operate again. Most notably being JobKeeper and Jobseeker: wage supplement schemes, investment impetus through depreciation deductions, credit guarantee scheme for SMEs, increasing the asset write-off threshold (Cassells et al., 2020).

Owing to Australian government's effective, timely, and actionable policy responses the economic downturn has been less pronounced in Australia than in many other economies, and Australia is now moving into a "COVID normal" phase of recovery (Child et al., 2020). As a crisis is an unexpected event, and so the key is to act upon it as quickly as possible, as entrepreneurship is integral to bounce back, which is what Australia did. Nevertheless, as Coronavirus is an ongoing crisis, research should continue in the direction of entrepreneurial policy responses and their implications.

SMEs in Australia

SMEs are an integral part of the Australian economy, as it is made up of 1000 s of them, which are vital for the economy and growth of the nation as employers, and as generators of value. According to the Australian Small Business and Family Enterprise Ombudsman, small businesses in Australia account for between "97.4 per cent and 98.4 per cent of all businesses". Furthermore, in 2018–2019, small businesses contributed almost \$418 billion to Gross Domestic Product (GDP) which accounts for more than 32% of Australia's total economy. Small businesses employ 41% of the workforce, which is almost 4.7 million people, thus making small businesses the largest employer (Simmons, 2020). It is therefore evident that SMEs in Australia are critical for growth and development in post-crisis recovery. Failure to support the SMEs could put the Australian economy at risk. Therefore, since the onset of this health crisis, the government has introduced and implemented policy responses aimed at addressing the needs of the SMEs (Albaz et al., 2020).

Research proposition 1 SMEs in Australia are integral for its growth and development in post-crisis recovery.

Overall, 70% of the businesses surveyed in mid-June 2020 by the Australian Bureau of Statistics (ABS), reported a decline in their revenues. Survey data also highlighted that there is a decline in business confidence and entrepreneurs are very uncertain about their future. In comparison to small retailers, larger retailers demonstrated strong growth in their sales (Lewis & Liu, 2020). In the first half of 2020, the unemployment rate rose from 5.2% in March to 7.4% in June, but all this would have been much worse without prompt policy initiatives to support businesses and their workforce (Lim et al., 2021).

However, the effects of the Coronavirus have been more pronounced in the hospitality industry and travel and tourism industry which includes restaurants, car rental companies, tour operators, arts and recreational services, accommodation, (hotels and motels), etc. SMEs being dominant in these sectors have received a severe blow from the outbreak of the Coronavirus and the measures to contain the spread of the virus (Rhodri, 2000). Therefore, despite government's policy measures to support the SMEs and their workforce, the closure of international borders had an instant negative consequence on international tourism. The impact on the travel and tourism industry was twofold, both from the loss of domestic business due to lockdown and the demise of international tourism due to border closures (Lim et al., 2021). Even though government policy measures are in place, the industry recovery will be slow in the short term, due to the ongoing fear revolving around COVID-19, federal government's cautious approach in opening international borders. However, the inbound travel restrictions are easing which could give some boost to the industry and the SMEs working in the industry (IBIS World, 2021).

Reflection on the Policy Response

There has been rising interest in entrepreneurship policy and one of the compelling forces behind this rising interest is the strong relationship between entrepreneurship and economic growth, development, and renewal. In the entrepreneurship literature, five types of policy interventions have been highlighted that could have an impact on entrepreneurial activity levels. "Type 1 interventions impact on the demand side of entrepreneurship (affecting the type, number and accessibility of entrepreneurial opportunities); Type 2 interventions impact on the supply of potential entrepreneurs (immigration policy, regional development policy); Type 3 interventions affect the availability of resources and knowledge for potential entrepreneurs (advice and counselling, direct financial support, venture capital and entrepreneurship education); Type 4 interventions shape entrepreneurial values in society (through the education system and the media); and Type 5 interventions alter the risk-reward profile of entrepreneurship by directing interventions at the decision-making process of individuals and their occupational choices (e.g. taxation, social security arrangements, labour market legislation, bankruptcy policy)" (Lundstrom & Stevenson, 2005, pp. 9–10).

Research proposition 2 The role of government is crucial in establishing an institutional framework at the country level to support businesses and entrepreneurs.

All the above-mentioned policy interventions suggest the role of government in establishing an institutional framework at the country level to support entrepreneurs. Therefore, governments in the developed economy are paying more and more attention to entrepreneurship policies because of their role in boosting entrepreneurial activity and economic performance. In 1999 GEM report highlighted that policy focus on entrepreneurship is crucial for three main reasons (Lundstrom & Stevenson, 2005):

- There is a positive relationship between new start-ups and economic growth and prosperity.
- New business contributes to employment generation in a major way, whereas large businesses shed jobs.
- The capability of a country to replenish the stock of businesses and jobs and to withstand the volatility and strain faced by small businesses will allow it to be well-positioned to compete effectively in the global economy.

Research proposition 3 Policy interventions have a crucial role to play in boosting entrepreneurial activity and economic performance.

Entrepreneurs and businesses exist in every society; however, it flourishes in a supportive environment. SMEs being an integral part of the Australian economy needed support more than ever due to the COVID-19 crisis and the lockdown which was imposed in mid-March 2020 to curtail the spread of the virus. Policies that are entrepreneurial in nature or that support entrepreneurship, are believed to be more innovative and futuristic in their approach (Ratten, 2021). The Australian government, therefore, acknowledged that this "once-in-a-century shock warrants an extraordinary level of support across the economy" which led them to announce policy measures to support the SMEs and their employees and keep the businesses afloat until the virus is contained and it's safe to operate again (budget.gov.au, 2020). Table 3.1 shows the ***response measures*** announced by the Federal government in March 2020 (Deloitte, 2020):

Apart from providing these response measures, the Australian government made sure that these relief measures or policy responses reach the businesses who require support and so the Australian government created a dedicated website on the available support measures for the businesses and also set up an SME hotline (Albaz et al., 2020).

The study by the Australian Small Business and Family Enterprise Ombudsman has highlighted "the number of businesses entering external voluntary administration declined sharply in March 2020 and has remained below 2019 levels" though the study acknowledges that "this is likely the result of financial support measures delivered in response to the

Table 3.1 Entrepreneurial support measures

Entrepreneurial support: Economic measures	*Targeted Outcomes*
Tax relief of up to $100,000 to support the eligible SMEs and non-for-profits with an aggregated turnover of under $50 million, with a minimum payment of $20,000	To assist the businesses with cash flow which in turn will assist in keeping the businesses afloat and maintain jobs
Support for business investment, by (1) increasing instant asset write-off from $30,000 to $150,000 and (2) a new time-limited 15-month investment incentive by accelerating depreciation deductions for businesses with an annual turnover of < $500 million (up from $50 million)	To provide a comprehensive safety net to businesses so that normal business operations can be resumed when the crisis has passed
Temporary increase in the threshold at which point creditors can issue a statutory demand on a company (and the time companies have to respond to statutory demands they receive) from $2000 to $20,000	
Support small businesses to retain apprentices and trainees, through a wage subsidy of 50% for nine months from January to September 2020	To avoid unemployment of skilled workers
JobKeeper payment: Wage subsidy	To support businesses in retaining their workforce
$1 billion to support communities, regions, and industries most significantly affected, including a $715 million package for the airline industry	To remove regulatory cost and ease the financial burden
A Coronavirus SME Guarantee Scheme will be introduced where the government will provide a 50% guarantee on new loans made by SMEs with a turnover of up to $50 million, for working capital purposes	To provide easy access to credit

Entrepreneurial support: Economic measures	*Targeted Outcomes*
Series of financial support measures (valued at $1.6 billion) for businesses: • Waiving of payroll tax • Bringing forward payroll tax cuts • Waiving fees and charges for small businesses • Employing additional cleaners for public infrastructure • Bringing forward maintenance • of public assets and capital works	To reduce the financial burden on small businesses and boost jobs

Source Author's own

crisis and temporary changes to insolvent trading protections" (Simmons, 2020). Prompt policy measures introduced in the early half of 2020 and flattening of the Coronavirus curve in the second half of 2020 led to economic recovery with GDP rebounding in the September quarter by 3.3%. Consumer confidence was also restored to an extent, as a 7.9% increase was reported in household consumption (Lim et al., 2021). By June 2020, it was reported that 61% of SMEs have accessed some sort of support measures (Cassells et al., 2020).

Research Proposition 4 Prompt government policy responses are needed to lead the economy into the recovery phase.

With the flattening of the virus curve, easing restrictions, and government decisive policy responses (in the first half) Australia moved to into a "COVID normal" phase of recovery. In this recovery phase, 13% of the small businesses reported that additional government support measures were required, whereas only seven per cent of medium and large businesses reported the need for additional support (Cassells et al., 2020). To further aid the recovery process of the SMEs, the Government introduced phase 2 policy response measures with a more targeted approach to help the businesses in their recovery phase. This clearly shows that the government is acting in an agile and iterative manner, adjusting its response measures as per the need of the hour.

Below are the ***recovery measures*** introduced in the latter half of 2020 (budget.gov.au, 2020):

- Extending the JobKeeper fund (with certain alterations), to support small businesses in retaining their employees.
- JobMaker Hiring Credit to encourage enterprises to hire new employees aged between 16 and 35.
- JobTrainer Fund to encourage apprenticeships and increase the availability of a skilled workforce.
- Supporting Business Investment to offer tax incentives to increase cash flow and support new investments.
- Infrastructure Stimulus: to support 40,000 jobs in the construction sector and improve cash flow in the economy.

All the above measures clearly show that they are introduced to provide direct support to the job seeker, young workers, and support to businesses. Even though Australia is on the path of recovery, the recovery rate is still slow and uneven as international border restrictions are still in place and will continue to be until late 2021, which is affecting a lot of SMEs in the travel and tourism industry. Therefore, very recently in March 2021, Prime Minister, Scott Morrison stated that now the focus on the policy will be to target regions, workers, and businesses that are still in distress. Hence the government announced, "The new Tourism Aviation Network Support (TANS) Program" to incentivise Australians to travel to "key domestic tourism areas". As per the program, discounts will be offered on airfares to encourage Australians to travel locally, this will in turn boost the local community and the businesses. This program is targeting 13 regional areas namely Cairns, Gold coast, the Sunshine Coast, the Whitsundays and Mackay region (Proserpine and Hamilton Island), Lasseter and Alice Springs, Devonport, and Burnie, Launceston, Avalon, Broome, Merimbula, and Kangaroo Island. (Prime Minister of Australia, 2021). Since it was introduced very recently the outcome of these response measures is yet to be seen and studied. It is therefore evident that policy introduction and implementation is an agile and iterative process.

Research Proposition 5 Policy introduction and implementation is an agile and iterative process.

Recommendations for Future Research

According to International Labour Organization, government response measures to support enterprises will mainly take place in three different phases: (1) reduction in economic activity due to lockdown measures to contain the spread of the virus; (2) reviving the business activity once the spread of the virus is curtailed; and (3) promoting enterprise resilience and sustainability (International Labour Organization, 2020). This means that all policy initiatives are location and time bound because policies are developed keeping in mind what is required in a specific time frame, and since COVID-19 is an ongoing crisis, therefore, there is a continuous need to study the impact of policy responses on the entrepreneurship phase by phase.

While this paper provides a link between the COVID-19 pandemic, entrepreneurship, and policy initiatives to support businesses especially SMEs. There is also a need to enrich the literature with wider research on entrepreneurship and associated policy initiative's (introduction, implementation, and outcome), as it would be useful to manage a future crisis.

Conclusion

The COVID-19 has affected the business world tremendously especially SMEs, however, its role in reviving the Australian economy cannot be ignored as there is a strong relationship between entrepreneurship and economic growth, development, and renewal. The role of government policy measures is therefore crucial in establishing an institutional framework at the country level to support businesses and entrepreneurs, which can be prominently seen in the case of Australia. Owing to its effective, timely, and actionable policy responses the economic downturn has been less pronounced in Australia than in many other economies, and Australia is now moving into a "COVID normal" phase of recovery.

References

Albaz, A., Mansour, T., & Schubert, J. (2020). *Setting up small and medium-size enterprises for restart and recovery.* https://www.mckinsey.com/industries/public-and-social-sector/our-insights/setting-up-small-and-medium-size-enterprises-for-restart-and-recovery. Accessed 10 Apr 2021.

budget.gov.au. (2020). *Economic Recovery Plan for Australia: COVID-19 Response Supporting Australians through the crisis.* https://budget.gov.au/2020-21/content/covid-19.htm. Accessed 11 Apr 2021.

Cassells, R., Duncan, A., Kiely, D., & Mavisakalyan, A. (2020). *Impact and response of businesses in Australia to COVID-19.* https://bcec.edu.au/assets/2020/07/BCEC-COVID19-Brief-7-Business-Impact-and-Response-_final.pdf. Accessed 10 Apr 2021.

Child, J., Dillon, R., Erasmus, E., & Johnson, J. (2020). *Collaboration in crisis: Reflecting on Australia's COVID-19 response.* https://www.mckinsey.com/industries/public-and-social-sector/our-insights/collaboration-in-crisis-reflecting-on-australias-covid-19-response. Accessed 10 Apr 2021.

Deloitte. (2020). *Whatever it takes COVID-19 policy responses in Australia.* https://www2.deloitte.com/content/dam/Deloitte/au/Documents/covid-19/deloitte-au-covid-19-dae-policy-responses.pdf. Accessed 10 Apr 2021.

Handley, E., 2020. *From Wuhan to Australia: A timeline of key events in the spread of the deadly coronavirus.* https://www.abc.net.au/news/2020-

01-29/coronavirus-timeline-from-wuhan-china-to-global-crisis/11903298?nw=0. Accessed 11 Apr 2021.
IBIS World. (2021). *Tourism in Australia – Market Research.* https://www.ibisworld.com/au/industry/tourism/1903/. Accessed 13 Apr 2021.
International Labour Organization. (2020). *I nterventions to support enterprises during the COVID-19 pandemic and recovery.* https://www.ilo.org/wcmsp5/groups/public/---ed_emp/---emp_ent/documents/publication/wcms_741870.pdf. Accessed 11 Apr 2021.
Lewis, M., & Liu, Q. (2020). *The COVID-19 Outbreak and Access to Small Business Finance.* https://www.rba.gov.au/publications/bulletin/2020/sep/the-covid-19-outbreak-and-access-to-small-business-finance.html. Accessed 10 Apr 2021.
Lim, G., Nguyen, V., Robinson, T., Tsiaplias, S., & Wang, J. (2021). The Australian Economy in 2020–21: The COVID-19 Pandemic and Prospects for Economic Recovery. *The Australian Economic Review, 54*(1), 5–18.
Liu, Y.-C., Kuo, R. L., & Shih, S. R. (2020). COVID-19: The first documented coronavirus pandemic in history. *Biomedical Journal, 43*(4), 328–333.
Lundstrom, A., & Stevenson, L. A. (2005). Introduction. In M. A. Boston (Ed.), *Entrepreneurship policy: Theory and practice* (pp. 1–40). Springer.
Prime Minister of Australia. (2021). *Tourism and Aviation's flight path to recovery.* https://www.pm.gov.au/media/tourism-and-aviations-flight-path-recovery. Accessed 11 Apr 2021.
Ratten, V. (2020). Coronavirus (Covid-19) and entrepreneurship: Cultural, lifestyle and societal changes. *Journal of Entrepreneurship in Emerging Economies, 13*(4), 747–761.
Ratten, V. (2021). COVID-19 and entrepreneurship: Future research directions. *Strategic Change, 30*(2), 91–98.
Rhodri, T. (2000). Small firms in the tourism industry: Some conceptual issues. *International Journal of Tourism Research, 2*(5), 345–353.
Simmons, D. (2020). *Ombudsman: Small business sector resilient through COVID-19 crisis.* https://www.businessnewsaustralia.com/articles/ombudsman--small-business-sector-resilient-through-covid-19-crisis.html. Accessed 10 Apr 2021.

CHAPTER 4

The Multiple Layers of Coopetition and Their Link with Sales Performance: Insights from Sporting Clubs in New Zealand

James M. Crick and Dave Crick

Introduction

Grounded in resource-based theory (Barney, 1991; Zollo & Winter, 2002), the objective of this chapter is to evaluate whether local-level coopetition, national-level coopetition, and organisation-level coopetition are positive drivers of sales performance; that is, in the context of sporting

J. M. Crick (✉)
School of Business and Economics, Loughborough University, Loughborough, UK
e-mail: j.m.crick@lboro.ac.uk

D. Crick
Telfer School of Management, University of Ottawa, Ottawa, ON, Canada

V. Ratten (ed.), *Oceania Entrepreneurship*,
https://doi.org/10.1007/978-981-16-7341-2_4

clubs within New Zealand. Throughout the wider cross-disciplinary literature, coopetition (cooperation among competitors) has been found to be a fundamental strategy consideration for various owner-managers (Bengtsson & Kock, 2000; Crick, 2019a; Granata et al., 2018). There are multiple definitions of coopetition (e.g., Bengtsson & Kock, 2014; Bouncken et al., 2015), but one capturing the value-adding nature of the strategy is that "coopetition refers to simultaneous competition and cooperation among firms with value creation intent" (Gnyawali & Charleton, 2018, p. 2514). That is, by working with industry rivals via a collaborative rather than individualistic business model (e.g., sharing equipment and knowledge), entrepreneurs can acquire new resources, capabilities, and opportunities that allow them to survive and grow within their markets (Crick, 2018a; Ritala et al., 2014). As such, it is not surprising that an established body of work surrounds the performance-enhancing benefits of coopetition, or similar activities, like alliances (Chetty & Wilson, 2003; Crick et al., 2021a; Ritala, 2012). However, there may be complexities (and potential "dark-sides") influencing the relationship between coopetition and organisational performance (Hoffmann et al., 2018; Shu et al., 2017). Therefore, the entrepreneurship community of researchers has signified that coopetition is advantageous when effectively managed, especially for small enterprises that have scarce resources and capabilities (Crick, 2019b; Dana et al., 2013).

That said, a considerable proportion of earlier work has signified that coopetition is a uni-dimensional variable that is comprised of cooperative and competitive issues, whereby it has been conceptualised, operationalised, and tested under one composite construct (e.g., Bouncken & Kraus, 2013; Bouncken et al., 2018; Crick & Crick, 2021a). This is a problem because an alternative perspective exists, suggesting coopetition is a multi-faceted variable, since organisations (small and large) can cooperate with their competitors across different regional areas and between product-markets[1] (Geldes et al., 2017; Rusko, 2011). To overcome this issue, Crick and Crick (2019) developed and validated a

[1] The multiple layers of the coopetition construct have been investigated in earlier studies, but focused on activities between organisations' departments, especially larger-sized companies with various functional areas (e.g., Ranganathan et al., 2018; Strese et al., 2016). As an illustration, Luo et al. (2006) found that "cross-functional coopetition" can lead to higher-levels of business performance (like in terms of customer satisfaction and financial metrics), especially when firms' owner-managers are able to learn about their markets. Alternatively, despite there being some research on the multiple-levels of coopetition (based on geographic and product-market factors), there are relatively few

multi-dimensional operationalisation of coopetition (namely, the COOP scale). Linking with their earlier qualitative study (see Crick & Crick, 2016a), they found that coopetition is comprised of three dimensions. First, local-level coopetition refers to entrepreneurs collaborating with their rivals within a close location (Felzensztein et al., 2014). Second, national-level coopetition is where decision-makers cooperate with their competitors in the same country, but are not restricted to any particular regional area (Crick, 2020; Gnyawali & Park, 2011). Third, organisation-level coopetition is the interplay between cooperation and competition, irrespective of geographic locations or key product-markets (Kock et al., 2010).

While Crick and Crick's (2019) study identified the multiple layers of coopetition activities, they overlooked how these different dimensions might influence firm-level success. It is therefore unclear whether the facets of their multi-dimensional operationalisation, respectively, lead to higher degrees of sales performance. This is important because research is needed to unpack the complexity of the coopetition construct (i.e., not examining the coopetition construct in uni-dimensional terms). This chapter therefore assesses the extent to which the three dimensions of the COOP scale (as per Crick & Crick, 2019) impact sales performance. If the existing body of knowledge continues to theorise, measure, and test coopetition is a composite variable (as per Bouncken & Kraus, 2013; Bouncken et al., 2018; Crick & Crick, 2021a), not only is the variance of this latent variable condensed (and minimised), but also, incorrect (or misguided) inferences could be made about the advantages and disadvantages of cooperating with competing enterprises (linking with Cadogan, 2012; Crick, 2021a). By addressing the previously mentioned research objective, three contributions are offered to the entrepreneurship literature:

1. Instead of conceptualising and operationalising coopetition as a uni-dimensional construct (as undertaken by Bouncken & Kraus, 2013; Bouncken et al., 2018; Crick & Crick, 2021a), the different forms of these strategies are unpacked, in terms of their potential influences on sales performance (building upon Rusko, 2011;

insights into how the different dimensions of these strategies impact sales performance (see, for example, Felzensztein et al., 2010; Kock et al., 2010; Granata et al., 2018).

Geldes et al., 2017; Crick et al., 2020a). This is an important contribution because if multi-faceted constructs are conceptualised, operationalised, and tested as composite variables, they lose their meaning and variance, which could lead to poor conclusions being made by researchers (as noted by Cadogan, 2012; Crick, 2021a). By using Crick and Crick's (2019) COOP scale, these drawbacks are reduced in respect of the coopetition construct. Indeed, these issues are examined in greater depth by undertaking a post-hoc test to evaluate the coopetition construct in a composite ("aggregated") form (similar to Cadogan et al., 2009). This demonstrates the importance of appreciating the multi-dimensionality of this latent variable (and to reinforce the appropriateness of testing the elements of the conceptual model in a "disaggregated" capacity).

2. Rather than utilising the resource-based view to solely examine its core (seminal) issues, such as the link between organisational resources/capabilities and business performance (as per Barney, 1991; Barney et al., 2011), the more recent aspects of this theoretical lens are investigated to highlight how cooperating with key stakeholders (here, competitors) is connected to this viewpoint (Barney, 2018; Sraha et al., 2020; Crick et al., 2021a). This is important, since the resource-based view has been adapted and debated over across the last thirty years (e.g., Barney, 2001; Priem & Butler, 2001; Chaudhry et al., 2019; Crick, 2021b). By using the seminal and recent aspects of resource-based theory, a "bigger picture" (i.e., with a higher degree of conceptual accuracy) is acknowledged when applying this perspective.
3. The multiple layers of coopetition are examined through the setting of non-mainstream (and smaller-sized) sporting clubs in New Zealand to provide a unique illustration of how these strategies can be managed by entrepreneurs to maximise their sales performance (extending Lorgnier & Su, 2014; Wemmer et al., 2016; Crick & Crick, 2021b). Sporting organisations provide an ideal empirical context for various entrepreneurial strategies because the operations of small entities within this highly influential sector are sometimes transferrable to mainstream environments (in line with Hodgkinson et al., 2012; Ratten, 2019; Ratten & Ferreira, 2017; Ratten & Ratten, 2011). In turn, these findings enhance a growing body of research that has focused on sports-focused entrepreneurial

behaviours in a range of countries (e.g., Ratten, 2012; Ratten & Tajeddini, 2019; Ratten & Thompson, 2020).

To make these three contributions, this chapter is divided as follows. First, the chapter is positioned in the context of the broader sports entrepreneurship literature. Second, pertinent studies surrounding the theoretical underpinnings are reviewed, leading to the development of the conceptual model. Third, the chosen methodology is described (a mainly quantitative research design). Fourth, the statistical results are outlined. Fifth, these results are discussed in relation to the extant literature. Sixth, the chapter ends with some implications for practitioners, together with several limitations and avenues for future research.

Context

Through the empirical context of small Taekwon-Do clubs in New Zealand, this chapter enhances the broader sports entrepreneurship literature. That is, entrepreneurial behaviours in a sporting environment have been approached in various respects. These include: studies on sports-oriented corporate social responsibility (Ratten & Babiak, 2010), social media in sports (Lopez-Carril et al., 2020), sports technology (Ratten, 2020a), sports-based internationalisation (Ratten, 2011a), how the COVID-19 pandemic has impacted the sports sector (Ratten, 2020b), educational issues in sports entrepreneurship (Ratten & Jones, 2018), family-owned sporting businesses (Ratten, 2021; Ratten & Dickson, 2021; Ratten & Li, 2021), sports-oriented team performance management (Ratten, 2009), digital sports ecosystems (Ratten & Thompson, 2020), customer value creation in sports (Ratten & Jones, 2020), policy issues in sporting contexts (Ratten, 2017), organising sports-related community events (Miragaia et al., 2018), and leadership in sports clubs (Ratten, 2015). Collectively, these research topics demonstrate how sports entrepreneurship is a varied domain, but surrounds the opportunity-driven behaviours that sporting organisations (small and large) use in their day-to-day and long-term activities (Ratten, 2012). This could be denoted as the innovative, risk-taking, and proactive actions that sporting entities (small and large—involving numerous stakeholders) use to design and execute performance-enhancing strategies (Ratten, 2011b; Ratten & Nanere, 2020). This chapter focuses on coopetition (as an entrepreneurial strategy) in the sports industry (building upon Crick &

Crick, 2016a). This is not the same as a "contribution to context", as it is anticipated that the findings from this investigation will be applicable to owner-managers in other sectors and countries.

Conceptual Model

Resource-Based Theory

Resource-based theory examines the connection between organisational resources/capabilities and business performance (Barney, 1991). Resources are tangible assets, including equipment, financial capital, and technological hardware, whereas, capabilities are intangible assets, such as knowledge and experience (Hills et al., 2008). This lens highlights that resources and capabilities fall under the value, rarity, inimitability, and non-substitutability (VRIN) framework, whereby, if entrepreneurs meet (or exceed) these factors, their tangible and intangible assets will yield a sustainable competitive advantage (Barney et al., 2011). A sustainable competitive advantage is just one measure of organisational performance given that entrepreneurs' objectives can vary over time; therefore, performance expectations may change to meet those evolving goals (Crick et al., 2018). Nevertheless, the "sustainable" nature of a competitive advantage pertains to companies (small and large) achieving long-term success; that is, resistant to the forces of the external market, like competitiveness and technological volatility (Vorhies & Morgan, 2005). However, in studies that do not undertake a longitudinal perspective, a popular benchmark is sales performance because it captures the degree to which entrepreneurs (regardless of whether their objectives are lifestyle-oriented or growth-oriented) have obtained revenues from their customers (Crick & Crick, 2016b; Crick et al., 2018; Jones et al., 2020). For this reason, this current investigation utilised sales performance as the outcome variable.

The seminal aspects of resource-based theory were devoted to examining internal issues (via the VRIN framework), not least of which, how decision-makers can acquire and exploit their resources and capabilities to yield higher-levels of performance (Zollo & Winter, 2002). Over time, this theoretical lens was expanded to account for various factors that entrepreneurs should navigate in their day-to-day and long-term operations. For instance, Barney (2001) debated with Priem and Butler (2001) about the future research directions surrounding resource-based theory. One area that they agreed on was that this perspective was focused on "inside the firm" issues, as it did not examine the market-level variables that might impact how organisations (small and large) implement their resources and capabilities into their short-term and long-term activities. Hence, Barney (2001) and Priem and Butler (2001) noted that these external factors should be incorporated into resource-based theory. This chapter highlights that coopetition (an external strategy involving under-resourced firms cooperating with their competitors) is connected with the seminal and extended themes of resource-based theory.[2] This perspective builds upon the recent work of Barney (2018), in which some under-resourced entrepreneurs are more likely to boost their performance if they network with key stakeholders (here, industry rivals). These themes underpinned the study's conceptual model outlined in Fig. 4.1.

Local-Level Coopetition and Sales Performance

Local-level coopetition is described as the degree to which entrepreneurs share resources and capabilities with their competitors within a close geographic proximity. For example, small businesses in regional clusters, like wine and other agricultural producers, might need to borrow certain pieces of equipment from nearby rivals or share knowledge to survive and prosper within their industries (Felzensztein et al., 2019; Geldes et al., 2017). If under-resourced entrepreneurs can acquire resources/capabilities from their competitors within the same region, they can combine them with their own assets to enhance performance, like via conserving costs or pursuing opportunities otherwise not available to them. That is, it could be harder to acquire and utilise certain resources from competitors that are larger distances away, such as rivals located on the other side of a country (Felzensztein et al., 2014; Granata et al., 2018; Telfer, 2001). Similarly, if decision-makers in under-resourced firms

[2] This chapter is underpinned by resource-based theory (e.g., Barney, 1991; Barney et al., 2011; Priem & Butler, 2001), but draws upon the wider entrepreneurship literature. Specifically, utilising studies positioned at the marketing/entrepreneurship interface that is also termed entrepreneurial marketing (see Morgan et al., 2015; Crick & Crick, 2018; Crick et al., 2020b). The reason being is that coopetition falls under this cross-disciplinary domain because it surrounds decision-makers engaging in innovative, proactive, and risk-taking behaviours used to create value for their customers (see Crick and Crick, 2016a; Crick, 2019b). Indeed, the entrepreneurial marketing literature has been approached in different respects, with various interpretations of these firm-wide actions (Crick & Crick, 2015; Crick et al., 2016; Hansen et al., 2020; Morris et al., 2002).

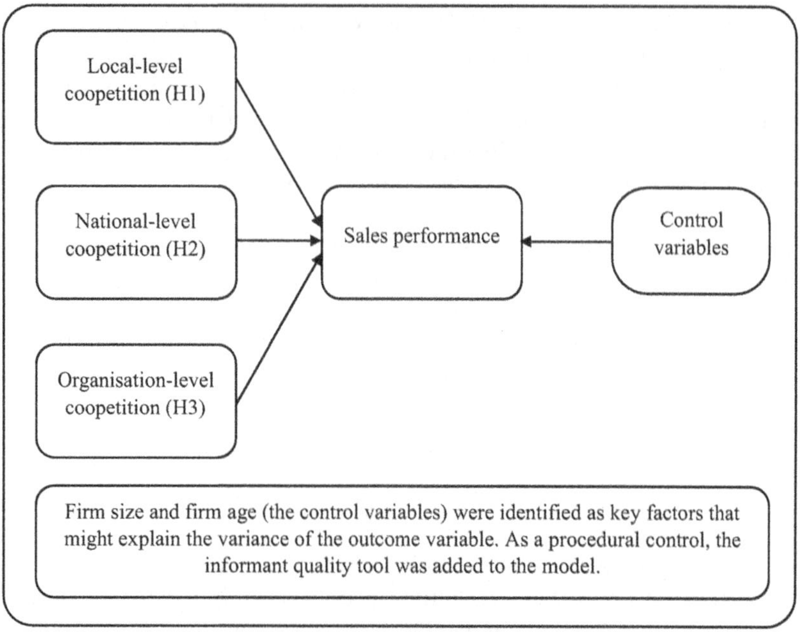

Fig. 4.1 Conceptual model

possess new capabilities from geographically close competitors, they might be able to use these intangible assets to create value for their customers in ways that might prove difficult if they were to compete under an individualistic business model (Crick et al., 2021b; Dana et al., 2013; Ratten, 2014). This is especially important for those that cannot afford (and do not have the time) to travel large distances to acquire resources and capabilities from their coopetition partners (Felzensztein et al., 2018; Crick, 2021c). Instead, they may develop social capital via informal "psychological contracts" based on trust with geographically close competitors for mutually beneficial purposes (Crick & Crick, 2021d). Thus, it stands to reason that:

H1. Higher-levels of local-level coopetition lead to increased sales performance.

National-Level Coopetition and Sales Performance

National-level coopetition refers to the extent to which decision-makers cooperate with their competitors within the same country, but across different regional areas (Crick & Crick, 2019). This form of coopetition has become relatively feasible, given that new technologies and modes of communication allow businesses (in various sectors) to collaborate with industry rivals across larger geographic distances (Crick et al., 2020a; Gnyawali & Park, 2011). National-level coopetition can involve competing under-resourced firms from different parts of a country working together through resource and capability-sharing activities (see Rusko, 2011). For instance, some smaller-sized and geographically dispersed firms opt to offer joint promotions to share costs and create "added-value" for their customers (Crick, 2015; Crick et al., 2021c). The rationale is that in certain circumstances, geographically distant firms are not direct rivals, such as when customers buy a product associated with a certain region and so competitive intensity is minimised (Crick & Crick, 2021d). This includes owner-managers collaborating with their rivals in ways that may extend to activities in foreign markets because of the high costs of operating internationally (Bengtsson & Kock, 2000; Crick, 2020). These combined resources and capabilities can allow entrepreneurs to promote their goods, services, and brands to their end-users (domestic and foreign) and reduce their overheads, together with branching out into new product-markets (Crick & Crick, 2020; Felzensztein & Deans, 2013; Felzensztein et al., 2010). Consequently, it follows that:

> H2. Higher-levels of national-level coopetition lead to increased sales performance.

Organisation-Level Coopetition and Sales Performance

Organisation-level coopetition pertains to the magnitude of cooperation with rivals across different geographic regions, but regardless of their key product-markets (Kock et al., 2010). For illustration purposes, Crick and Crick (2019) found that smaller-sized rival sporting entities (e.g., martial arts clubs) collaborate to obtain new resources, capabilities, and opportunities to boost their success. However, organisation-level coopetition applies to domestic and international product-markets, with some instances being smaller-sized clubs working with competitors possessing a large product-market overlap or those that are indirect rivals (consistent with Chetty & Wilson, 2003). By cooperating with rivals exhibiting a range of product-market overlaps, smaller-sized businesses can receive new abilities/opportunities that will help them to deliver value for their target markets (domestically and internationally) and how to conserve costs (Crick & Crick, 2019; Felzensztein et al., 2018). Accordingly, it is anticipated that:

> H3. Higher-levels of organisation-level coopetition lead to increased sales performance.

Control Variables

Other than a procedural control factor (as described later), the outcome variable (here, sales performance) was controlled for firm size and firm age. Linking with resource-based theory, together with the wider entrepreneurship literature, owner-managers that possess greater resources and capabilities (even in small businesses) are more likely to yield higher-levels of performance (domestically and/or internationally depending on products-markets served) than those with fewer assets (Barney et al., 2011; Crick & Crick, 2016c; Crick, 2021d). For this reason, firm size was modelled as a control path. Additionally, resource-based theory (and related conceptual issues within the existing body of knowledge) considers various ways that enterprises (small and large) can be successful other than scale-related issues (Barney, 2018; Crick & Crick, 2014; Jones & Rowley, 2011; Zollo & Winter, 2002). For instance, older organisations can sometimes leverage their heritage, such as social capital developed over time, to out-perform younger competitors (Vorhies et al., 2011). Hence, firm age controlled the outcome variable. The chosen methodology employed is described as follows.

Methods

Population of Interest

An ideal setting for coopetition-based research is a sector that is active in cooperative and competitive activities (Crick & Crick, 2020). That is, coopetition involves organisations (small and large) cooperating with their competitors for higher-levels of success (Bouncken & Kraus, 2013;

Ritala et al., 2014), meaning that it is important to select an industry (and country) context where these collaborative and rivalrous forces are at play. For example, the global wine industry has been used to investigate coopetition because smaller-sized vineyards and wineries are active in coopetition strategies, such as sharing tools and information for quality control purposes, or pooling assets to enter new domestic and international markets (Crick, 2018b; Crick & Crick, 2021c). Equally, the sporting industry is well-known for its coopetition activities. As an illustration, Lorgnier and Su (2014) found that small nautical clubs in France depend on working with their rivals to access knowledge, promote key regions, and for acquiring critical information. For this reason, the researchers selected non-mainstream (and smaller-sized) sporting organisations (Taekwon-Do clubs) in New Zealand to test the elements of the conceptual model. To clarify, Taekwon-Do is a Korean martial art that has been immersed in the ongoing political volatility between North Korea and South Korea, together with their respective allies (Hong, 2011; Merkel, 2008).

There are two main forms of the sport (which have different spellings), namely, the International Taekwon-Do Federation (ITF) and the World Taekwondo Federation (WTF), as well as various break-away bodies (Crick & Crick, 2016a). To access the necessary empirical data, the researchers worked with the senior leaders of an ITF governing body in New Zealand with 262 instructors and around 3500 members (their names and details are not reported for ethical reasons). Small Taekwon-Do clubs were deemed to be suitable for evaluating coopetition strategies because they tend to be collaborative via sharing equipment and information, but also, are competitive through members operating in rivalrous capacities to boost the performance of their own clubs (Crick & Crick, 2021b). The sporting context was anticipated to be transferrable to wider contexts (following Ratten, 2016; Hodgkinson et al., 2012; Ratten & Tajeddini, 2019; Jones et al., 2019; Ratten & Thompson, 2020; Thukral & Ratten, 2021). The researchers selected Taekwon-Do instructors as the key informants. The reason being is that these individuals are typically the main decision-makers within their clubs (Ahn et al., 2009). Put another way, Taekwon-Do instructors (in small clubs) were expected to possess the "correct" knowledge to answer the questions pertaining to the measures of the constructs within the conceptual model.

Preliminary Qualitative Stage

To ensure that the selected operationalisations (as described later) were "accurately" adapted towards the sporting setting, 25 semi-structured field interviews were undertaken with senior leaders of the earlier-mentioned ITF governing body in New Zealand, as well as with Taekwon-Do instructors. These semi-structured interviews lasted around sixty minutes and were used to explore some examples of local-level coopetition, national-level coopetition, and organisation-level coopetition—and their respective links with sales performance (building upon Felzensztein et al., 2019; Rusko, 2011; Telfer, 2001). Indeed, the researchers were informed that although the ITF governing body operated on a "not-for-profit" basis, the individual clubs had the autonomy to turn profits if their owner-managers wished (similar to Gallagher & Mitchell, 2016). To analyse the qualitative data, the transcripts were manually coded for three pre-determined themes (one for each of the hypothesised paths) (see Crick, 2021e). Furthermore, the constant comparison technique was employed to continually assess the data for re-occurring themes (Suddaby, 2006). The preliminary qualitative stage was primarily used to adapt the measurement scales to the chosen empirical context. Hence, such qualitative data were not utilised to explain the statistical results.

Survey Data Collection

The core research method was an electronic survey designed through Qualtrics. After this, the pre-testing stage took place with a sample of knowledgeable academics ($n = 10$) and practitioners ($n = 20$) (Dana & Dana, 2005). The interviewees at the pre-testing stage signified that the survey was clear, for which no changes were necessary. This led the researchers proceeding to the pilot study ($n = 31$) to check the preliminary measurement scales and descriptive statistics—revealing no problems (Hunt et al., 1982). Next, the core data collection stage was launched ($n = 80$). Since the operationalisations were identical between the pilot study and core study, the two datasets were merged (31 plus 80, $n = 111$) (Crick & Crick, 2021d). The 111 observations (as a proportion of 262 instructors) accounted for a 42.366% response rate.[3] This was respectable and was explained by the survey being very short, interactive, and engaging for the respondents (Newby et al., 2003). Furthermore, the senior leaders of the ITF governing body endorsed (with no pressure enforced) this study and encouraged responses. The research team tested for non-response bias by "running" t-tests for each latent variable across the first and second 50% of the observations. The non-significant t-values for all constructs were indicative of the statistical results being unaffected by response bias (Armstrong & Overton, 1977).

Measures

The constructs within the conceptual model were operationalised and adapted as follows. First, the different forms of the coopetition construct—local-level coopetition (LLC), national-level coopetition (NLC), and organisation-level coopetition (OLC)—were measured using the COOP scale (Crick & Crick, 2019; Crick, 2021b). This involved seven-point Likert scales, each with four items, ranging from: 1 = very strongly disagree to 7 = very strongly agree. Second, sales performance (SALES) was captured on a nine-point interval scale, with three items, ranging from: 1 = extremely dissatisfied to 9 = extremely satisfied (Morgan et al., 2009; Vorhies & Morgan, 2005). Third, firm size (SIZE) was operationalised through the total number of members in each Taekwon-Do club (Crick & Crick, 2021b). Fourth, firm age (AGE) was operationalised via the number of years since the Taekwon-Do clubs were established (Vorhies et al., 2011). Fifth, as an instrument for certain robustness checks (as described later), the survey ended with an informant quality tool (INQ), which was captured on a seven-point Likert scale, with five items, ranging from: 1 = very strongly disagree to 7 = very strongly agree (Crick, 2020). Natural logarithms were used to transform the single indicators to reduce their variances (Crick & Crick, 2021e).

[3] This chapter is part of a wider research project involving smaller-sized Taekwon-Do clubs in New Zealand. However, this dataset with 111 observations, has not been used elsewhere.

Scale Purification

To purify the multi-item measures, three exploratory factor analysis models (with different extraction and rotation specifications) were "run" using SPSS 25[4] (Fabrigar et al., 1999; Hamzah et al., 2021; Peterson, 2000; Stewart, 1981). Since no concerns existed with the multi-item scales, no measurement items were deleted. These tests showed that the indicators for local-level coopetition, national-level coopetition, organisation-level coopetition, sales performance, and the informant quality tool loaded onto five factors, with no cross-factor loadings (Table 4.1). The Kaiser–Meyer–Olkin (KMO) test of sampling adequacy was sufficient (0.755), as were the results from Bartlett's test of sphericity (χ^2 = 2360.944; *df* = 190; Sig. = 0.000). Hence, enough survey responses had been collected to test the elements of the conceptual model (Crick & Crick, 2021e). Additionally, each exploratory factor analysis model explained a reasonably high degree of variance. That is, model 1 was 76.947%, model 2 was 82.344%, and model 3 was 76.322%.

Model-Testing

During the model-testing stage, SPSS 25 was utilised to conduct an ordinary least squares (OLS) multiple regression analysis (alongside examining the bivariate correlation coefficients, descriptive statistics, and final scale reliabilities of the constructs). This approach was chosen because there were several independent variables (including the controls) and one outcome variable (Crick & Crick, 2019). In doing so, the research team recorded the unstandardised and standardised regression coefficients, coupled with their standard errors, *t*-values, and significance-levels (Morgan et al., 2009). The model fit summary was examined, with a focus on the adjusted R^2 to identify the percentage of variance of sales performance (the outcome variable) explained by the independent variables (Crick, 2021c).

[4] Before the scale purification process took place, the small amount of missing data were treated via expectation maximisation (see Enders, 2003). This involved replacing the few missing values with the mean for each latent variable (as per Crick, 2018c).

Table 4.1 Scale purification stage

	Model 1: components (generalised least squares extraction and a quartimax rotation)					*Model 2: components (principal components analysis extraction and a varimax rotation)*					*Model 3: components (maximum likelihood extraction and an equamax rotation)*				
Items	*1*	*2*	*3*	*4*	*5*	*1*	*2*	*3*	*4*	*5*	*1*	*2*	*3*	*4*	*5*
LLC_1	**0.935**	0.149	0.009	0.150	0.097	**0.913**	0.144	0.160	0.162	0.098	**0.919**	0.162	0.152	0.182	0.105
LLC_2	**0.938**	0.174	0.003	0.132	0.035	**0.913**	0.150	0.194	0.164	0.049	**0.939**	0.181	0.154	0.164	0.041
LLC_3	**0.838**	0.228	0.309	0.053	0.039	**0.817**	0.312	0.243	0.055	0.030	**0.711**	0.308	0.328	0.085	0.046
LLC_4	**0.827**	0.233	0.253	0.067	0.043	**0.833**	0.284	0.215	0.052	0.046	**0.709**	0.314	0.276	0.099	0.054
NLC_1	0.155	**0.698**	0.156	0.121	0.084	0.093	**0.817**	0.144	0.151	0.077	0.108	**0.713**	0.159	0.133	0.081
NLC_2	0.230	**0.845**	0.192	0.124	0.120	0.209	**0.845**	0.191	0.127	0.140	0.157	**0.885**	0.203	0.139	0.109
NLC_3	0.237	**0.644**	0.083	0.110	0.097	0.215	**0.787**	0.048	0.082	0.015	0.218	**0.639**	0.106	0.124	0.086
NLC_4	0.266	**0.923**	0.115	0.088	0.081	0.252	**0.847**	0.192	0.091	0.084	0.240	**0.855**	0.181	0.114	0.075
OLC_1	0.219	0.235	**0.875**	–0.0062	0.004	0.112	0.301	**0.823**	–0.096	0.011	0.089	0.262	**0.869**	–0.062	0.005
OLC_2	0.175	0.220	**0.817**	–0.067	–0.026	0.053	0.242	**0.869**	–0.081	–0.027	0.082	0.190	**0.884**	–0.067	–0.025
OLC_3	0.431	0.193	**0.497**	–0.016	0.025	0.345	0.104	**0.787**	0.008	0.054	0.415	0.153	**0.618**	–0.009	0.020
OLC_4	0.390	0.060	**0.451**	0.111	–0.055	0.325	–0.049	**0.741**	0.141	–0.050	0.367	0.017	**0.540**	0.119	–0.056
SALES_1	0.071	0.161	0.025	**0.815**	–0.121	0.030	0.154	0.047	**0.890**	–0.087	0.021	0.152	0.042	**0.822**	–0.111
SALES_2	0.149	0.127	0.015	**0.974**	–0.105	0.132	0.131	0.041	**0.938**	–0.113	0.109	0.114	0.042	**0.982**	–0.091
SALES_3	0.214	0.079	–0.172	**0.804**	–0.064	0.195	0.103	–0.131	**0.879**	–0.040	0.192	0.102	–0.133	**0.812**	–0.055
INQ_1	0.169	0.054	–0.160	–0.088	**0.744**	0.182	–0.032	–0.060	–0.053	**0.839**	0.181	0.055	–0.085	–0.091	**0.740**
INQ_2	0.106	0.063	–0.082	–0.088	**0.900**	0.090	0.050	–0.023	–0.053	**0.953**	0.098	0.097	–0.047	–0.099	**0.886**
INQ_3	0.038	0.080	–0.056	–0.085	**0.847**	0.014	0.068	–0.010	–0.029	**0.901**	0.026	0.111	–0.041	–0.097	**0.834**
INQ_4	0.006	0.061	0.089	–0.039	**0.987**	–0.009	0.105	0.061	–0.076	**0.942**	–0.009	0.074	0.079	–0.054	**0.977**
INQ_5	–0.045	0.067	0.096	–0.019	**0.959**	–0.061	0.122	0.031	–0.060	**0.927**	–0.071	0.084	0.075	–0.034	**0.961**

To extract the strongest operationalisations for each multi-item latent variable (considering the subsequent assessments for reliability and validity), the research team set 0.450 as a "cut-off" value for the factor loadings (noting that there is not a single-agreed way to determine what these scores should be). These extracted values are presented in a bold font. As per standard practice, the single-item scales (SIZE and AGE) did not feature in the exploratory factor analysis models. These extraction and rotation approaches were chosen based on several earlier studies (namely, Fabrigar et al., 1999; Hamzah et al., 2021; Peterson, 2000; Stewart, 1981). Since the factor loadings were comparable across all three models, there is no evidence to suggest that these scales were "incorrectly" retained.

Reliability and Validity

Through SPSS 25, reliability was examined via the Cronbach's alpha coefficients (α) of the multi-item scales—which were all greater than 0.700 (Churchill Jr., 1979). Furthermore, because the multi-item measures were in excess of the minimum benchmarks, the single-indicators were assumed to be of a reliable standard (Crick, 2018c). Validity was assessed in different respects. Specifically, face validity was checked through pre-testing the survey with a sample of expert academics and practitioners (Dana & Dana, 2005). In addition, face validity was assured through the informant quality scale (Crick, 2020). This revealed that the participants were qualified to complete the survey (with a mean score of 5.683). Content validity existed because all operationalisations were established (Peter, 1981). Discriminant validity was evaluated through the exploratory factor analysis models (via SPSS 25). That is, as the five multi-item constructs loaded onto distinct components (across the three approaches), there is evidence to suggest that these latent variables were significantly different to one another (Farrell & Rudd, 2009).

Common Method Bias

There are various ways to assess common method bias (as noted by Crick & Crick, 2019; Sraha et al., 2020). In this current investigation, the electronic survey was carefully designed to make it short, engaging, and interactive for the respondents (following Podsakoff et al., 2003). For instance, different colour schemes and scale layouts were used to help ensure that the key informants answered the questions (Crick, 2018c). As a more stringent evaluation, the research team used SPSS 25 to conduct the marker variable technique. This involved "running" two correlation matrices—a bivariate correlation matrix with all latent variables within the conceptual model (after they were purified) and another with the same constructs, but controlling for the informant quality tool (a partial correlation matrix). The informant quality tool was selected as the marker variable because it was theoretically unrelated to any other construct within the conceptual model (Crick et al., 2021a). The differences between the two correlation matrices were calculated and averaged. As the mean value was very low ($r = 0.008$), there is evidence to suggest that a common method factor did not provide bias (Lindell & Whitney,

2001). Furthermore, the informant quality tool had a relatively high standard deviation (0.722), allowing it to be employed as the marker variable.[5]

Post-Hoc Test

After evaluating the research hypotheses and control paths, a post-hoc test was employed to unpack the statistical results (Cadogan et al., 2009). The reason being is that owing to the considerable volume of work that surrounds uni-dimensional measures of coopetition (e.g., Bouncken & Kraus, 2013; Bouncken et al., 2018; Crick & Crick, 2021a), it was helpful to examine this latent variable in an "aggregated" (rather than "disaggregated") form—to determine whether this construct yields a positive and significant link with sales performance. For clarity, it is unwise to conceptualise, operationalise, and test multi-dimensional variables as composite constructs (Cadogan, 2012; Crick, 2021a). Yet, for exploratory purposes, a composite notion (the COOP scale) was used to demonstrate the importance of investigating the multiple layers of coopetition strategies and their respective associations with sales performance. Hence, if during the core model-testing stage, one (or more) dimension(s) of the COOP scale had no connection with sales performance, but if averaged, a positive and significant link was found, the evidence would signify that composite variables have considerable drawbacks. This involved an OLS multiple regression analysis (using SPSS 25), with sales performance as the outcome variable; also, coopetition (a composite measure of local-level coopetition, national-level coopetition, and organisation-level coopetition), firm size, firm age, and the informant quality tool as the independent variables. During the OLS multiple regression analysis, the researchers recorded the same outputs as within the main model-testing stage (Morgan et al., 2009; Crick, 2021c). The statistical results follow in the next section.

[5] There are different ways that the marker variable technique can be employed in multivariate statistical research (Lindell & Whitney, 2001; Morgan et al., 2015). In this chapter, the informant quality tool was included in the model-testing stage—as an extension of the marker variable technique (similar to Crick & Crick, 2019). This helped the researchers to monitor its impact on sales performance.

Statistical Results

The bivariate correlation coefficients displayed the underlying associations between the purified constructs, alongside their descriptive statistics and final scale reliabilities (Table 4.2).

Turning to the core model-testing stage, during the OLS multiple regression analysis, local-level coopetition and national-level coopetition yielded positive and significant relationships with sales performance. Hence, H1 and H2 were supported. That said, organisation-level coopetition had a negative, but non-significant link with sales performance. As such, no support existed for H3. As for the main control variables, firm size and firm age produced non-significant paths, whereas, the informant quality tool (the procedural control path—as a robustness check) was negatively and significantly related to sales performance. Moreover, the adjusted R^2 showed that 11.900% of the variance of sales performance was explained, together with a significant model fit summary (F-statistic = 3.482; Sig. = 0.004). The OLS multiple regression analysis is displayed in Table 4.3.

Regarding the post-hoc test, the composite COOP scale yielded a positive and significant association with sales performance. Additionally, like the main model-testing stage, similar results were found for firm size, firm age, and the informant quality tool (Table 4.4). Indeed, the adjusted R^2 revealed that 7.900% of the variance of sales performance was explained by the independent variables, with a significant model fit summary (F-statistic = 3.345; Sig. = 0.013). To stress an earlier point, the post-hoc test was employed for exploratory purposes—to demonstrate how an "aggregated" approach can distort certain statistical results. That is, it symbolises how empirical findings can vary if researchers "run" composite measures of multi-dimensional constructs. These results are discussed in the following section.

Table 4.2 Bivariate correlation coefficients, descriptive statistics, and scale reliabilities

Constructs	*1*	*2*	*3*	*4*	*5*	*6*	*7*	*8*
1. LLC	**0.950**							
2. NLC	0.473**	**0.898**						
3. OLC	0.473**	0.382**	**0.868**					
4. SALES	0.262**	0.267**	0.030	**0.909**				
5. SIZE	–0.038	0.008	–0.117	0.124†	–			
6. AGE	–0.118	0.071	0.095	–0.076	–0.138†	–		
7. INQ	0.112	0.156*	0.022	–0.127†	0.068	– 0.054	**0.951**	
8. COOP	0.887**	0.763**	0.753**	0.245**	–0.059	0.004	0.124†	–
Mean	4.343	4.895	3.505	5.028	4.154	3.417	5.683	4.248
Standard deviation	1.059	0.818	0.783	1.539	0.634	0.296	0.722	0.707
Minimum	1.000	1.000	1.000	1.000	1.390	2.200	3.800	2.000
Maximum	7.000	7.000	6.250	9.000	5.740	3.850	7.000	6.750

†$p < 0.100$; *$p < 0.050$; **$p < 0.010$; (one-sided tests). The composite coopetition construct (COOP) was "run" as part of the post-hoc test. That is, it is appreciated that some of these correlations were quite large. However, these were only for statistically (and conceptually) connected latent variables, such as COOP and the dimensions of this multi-dimensional operationalisation—which would be expected to produce high (and significant) correlation coefficients. Hence, no concerns were visible in this capacity. The Cronbach's alpha coefficients (α) are presented on the diagonal of the bivariate correlation matrix in a bold font

Table 4.3 OLS multiple regression analysis (main model-testing stage)

Constructs	*β*	*Standard errors*	*Beta*	t-*values*	*Sig*
LLC	0.350	0.162	0.241	2.158	0.033
NLC	0.461	0.199	0.245	2.321	0.022
OLC	–0.305	0.207	–0.155	-1.468	0.145
SIZE	0.291	0.221	0.120	1.316	0.191
AGE	–0.232	0.483	–0.045	–0.481	0.631
INQ	–0.424	0.194	–0.199	-2.185	0.031
Model fit					
R^2	0.167				
Adjusted R^2	0.119				
F-statistic	3.482				
Sig	0.004				

The critical *t*-value was 1.645 (5%, one-sided because the paths were directional). The outcome variable was SALES, whereby, *β* denotes the unstandardised regression coefficients and the beta-values were the standardised regression coefficients.

Table 4.4 OLS multiple regression analysis (post-hoc test)

Constructs	*β*	*Standard errors*	*Beta*	t-*values*	*Sig*
COOP	0.599	0.201	0.275	2.974	0.004
SIZE	0.345	0.225	0.142	1.535	0.128
AGE	–0.349	0.486	–0.067	–0.726	0.469
INQ	-0.371	0.197	–0.174	-1.880	0.063
Model fit					
R^2	0.112				
Adjusted R^2	0.079				
F-statistic	3.345				
Sig	0.013				

The critical *t*-value was 1.645 (5%, one-sided because the paths were directional). The outcome variable was SALES, whereby, *β* denotes the unstandardised regression coefficients and the beta-values were the standardised regression coefficients.

Discussion

Grounded in resource-based theory (Barney, 1991; Zollo & Winter, 2002), the objective of this chapter was to evaluate whether local-level coopetition, national-level coopetition, and organisation-level coopetition are positive drivers of sales performance. After undertaking a mainly quantitative investigation using survey responses from 111 small Taekwon-Do clubs in New Zealand (with such data passing all major robustness checks), the following seven discussion points are raised. First, local-level coopetition yielded a positive and significant link with sales performance (supporting Telfer, 2001; Granata et al., 2018; Crick et al., 2021b). This signifies that if entrepreneurs cooperate with their rivals within a close location, they can boost their sales performance through accessing new resources, capabilities, and opportunities (Dana et al., 2013; Felzensztein et al., 2019; Geldes et al., 2017; Ratten, 2014). Second, national-level coopetition had a positive and significant relationship with sales performance (reinforcing Gnyawali & Park, 2011; Crick et al., 2020a). This suggests that if owner-managers do not restrict their coopetition partnerships to small-scale geographic distances, they can increase their sales performance (Crick & Crick, 2020; Felzensztein & Deans, 2013; Felzensztein et al., 2010; Gnyawali & Charleton, 2018).

Third, one facet of the COOP scale was negatively and non-significantly connected to sales performance, namely, organisation-level coopetition (somewhat in contrast to Chetty & Wilson, 2003; Kock et al., 2010). This surprising result could be explained through smaller-sized sporting clubs not needing to cooperate with competitors across different product-markets to the same extent as mainstream enterprises. For instance, while there could be some value in working with Karate or Judo clubs (as per Crick & Crick, 2016a), these inter-firm networks might not be advantageous. It appears that local-level coopetition and national-level coopetition are more effective for entrepreneurs (vis-à-vis, organisation-level coopetition) because these activities assist them to increase their sales performance. The unsupported third hypothesised path builds upon a growing body of literature that has indicated that coopetition activities are more likely to drive particular assessments of success across different geographic proximities (Dana et al., 2013; Felzensztein et al., 2014; Granata et al., 2018), as opposed to between product-markets (as per Crick & Crick, 2019). These findings highlight two specific forms of coopetition that are likely to enhance sales performance, rather than certain decidedly vague conceptualisations and operationalisations in some earlier studies (building on Bouncken & Kraus, 2013; Bouncken et al., 2018; Crick & Crick, 2021a).

Fourth, as for the control variables, firm size and firm age had non-significant linkages with sales performance (somewhat challenging Morgan et al., 2009; Vorhies et al., 2011). These results imply that these constructs do not play a key role in driving entrepreneurs' success. For firm size, the existing body of knowledge (not least of which resource-based theory) suggests that larger-sized entities have a greater potential to yield higher-levels of sales performance than small players in their markets (Barney et al., 2011; Vorhies & Morgan, 2005). It might be that more resources and capabilities (coupled with a larger "workforce") do not necessarily facilitate such performance outcomes. As for firm age, resource-based theory (and the wider entrepreneurship literature) signifies that certain older companies can out-perform younger competitors due to having "time on their side", with experience in their sectors to learn about the best (and worst) ways to deliver value to their end-users (Crick, 2020; Vorhies et al., 2011). With a non-significant finding, it could be that firm age is not a key driver of sales performance—potentially because older enterprises are less agile to satisfy their customers' wants and needs, with restrictive and bureaucratic practices and systems (Jones & Rowley, 2011). It appears that certain core variables (local-level coopetition and national-level coopetition) are more likely to explain the variance of sales performance than the control factors (Geldes et al., 2017; Rusko, 2011).

Fifth, by underpinning the conceptual model with resource-based theory, strong conceptualisations were utilised. That is, while seminal aspects of resource-based theory examined the link between organisational resources/capabilities and company performance (Barney, 1991; Zollo & Winter, 2002), more recent aspects of the theoretical lens examine broader issues about how entrepreneurs operate within their markets. For example, the pivotal debate between Barney (2001) and Priem and Butler (2001) focused on market-level factors that could impact business performance (extending the VRIN framework). Likewise, Barney (2018) argued that some owner-managers network with key stakeholders (here, rivals) to achieve their objectives. Thus, the broader themes of resource-based theory enabled this chapter to draw upon networking issues and relate them to coopetition as a key entrepreneurial strategy. This theoretical perspective is highly relevant to the ways that decision-makers in under-resourced companies can combine their own resources and capabilities with those acquired from their rivals (alongside forging stronger networks) to boost their sales performance (see Ritala, 2012; Crick, 2021b).

Sixth, referring to the post-hoc test, when the coopetition construct was measured as a composite variable (via the COOP scale), it was found to have a positive and significant relationship with sales performance (supplementing Crick & Crick, 2019). In principle, this was an expected result because coopetition activities have been noted to be performance-enhancing entrepreneurial behaviours, including conceptualisations underpinned by resource-based theory (see Ritala, 2012; Dana et al., 2013; Bengtsson & Kock, 2014; Granata et al., 2018; Felzensztein et al., 2019). Yet, after breaking down the elements of the COOP scale, the main model-testing stage had mixed results, whereby, two facets were significant (and positive) drivers of sales performance and one was non-significant (and negative). Hence, it can be an unwise (and inaccurate) decision to conceptualise, operationalise, and test multi-dimensional constructs as uni-dimensional variables (Crick, 2021a). This result reinforces Cadogan's (2012) arguments about a market orientation (the organisation-wide implementation of the marketing concept and creation of superior customer value), with new evidence pertaining to the coopetition construct. This should be acknowledged by entrepreneurship researchers when studying coopetition in the years to come.

Seventh, as a final discussion point, the empirical context for this chapter enhanced the prior contributions to theory. Sporting organisations are well-known for being entrepreneurial, in terms of their innovative and proactive behaviours, together with their tendencies to take calculated risks (see Ratten & Ratten, 2011; Ratten, 2012; Jones et al., 2019; Ratten & Thompson, 2020; Thukral & Ratten, 2021). As such, the chosen setting of smaller-sized Taekwon-Do clubs in New Zealand revealed how these decision-makers are active in coopetition strategies and use them to increase their sales performance (extending Crick & Crick, 2016a). This emphasises that sports clubs have the potential to shape academic theory in entrepreneurial research (as per Ratten, 2016; Ratten & Ferreira, 2017; Ratten & Tajeddini, 2019). In this current investigation, coopetition was not only a performance-enhancing strategy, but also, is comprised of multiple dimensions. On that note, it is advisable for academics to conceptualise, operationalise, and test the coopetition construct as a multi-faceted notion. Put another way, if coopetition is examined in uni-dimensional terms, scholars could make poor conclusions because they have incorrectly theorised, measured, and evaluated this latent variable (linking with Cadogan, 2012; Crick, 2021a). Some practitioner implications are offered in the subsequent section.

Practitioner Implications

This chapter offers some implications for practitioners:

1. Entrepreneurs in under-resourced, smaller-sized enterprises might consider cooperating with their competitors within a close location (local-level coopetition). These relationships can help them to acquire new tangible and intangible assets (and opportunities) that are likely to boost their sales performance.
2. Owner-managers are advised to extend social networks and collaborate with appropriate industry rivals across a variety of regional areas (national-level coopetition). In doing so, they can increase their performance opportunities, while not restricting their prospective networks to a certain (fixed/localised) geographic area.
3. There can be risks associated with engaging in coopetition strategies with partners that operate across different product-markets (organisation-level coopetition). These activities could be a hindrance on entrepreneurs' time, whereby, they would be better served if they engaged in local-level coopetition and/or national-level coopetition.
4. Despite the merits of coopetition, these strategies have the potential to be challenging for decision-makers. If owner-managers engage in "too little" or "too much" of these strategies, there is a fair chance that they might lose vital knowledge and experience tensions with their coopetition partners. Consequently, the somewhat fragile balance between cooperation and competition must be maintained. Effective management of this social capital should take place, not only by teaming up with appropriate rivals, but also regarding recruitment, training and incentivising members of firms in order to share an entrepreneur's mindset regarding the merits of coopetition.
5. Decision-makers must appreciate that coopetition does not exist in one form. Instead, there are multiple ways that they can work with their industry rivals (across different regional areas and between product-markets). By appreciating the facets of coopetition, they can effectively navigate the risks and potential rewards of these strategies.

Collectively, these practical recommendations are designed to assist smaller-sized enterprises to engage in performance-enhancing coopetition strategies. Some limitations and avenues for future research are presented as follows.

Limitations and Avenues for Future Research

Although this chapter contributed to the broader entrepreneurship literature, there are several limitations and avenues for future research:

1. While the response rate was respectable (42.366%), the final sample size was quite small ($n = 111$). Nonetheless, key statistical tests were conducted to check whether enough survey responses had been collected (identifying no concerns). Scholars are advised to replicate this study with a larger sample size to produce generalisable results.
2. The empirical context was rather specific, namely, small Taekwon-Do clubs in New Zealand. This setting was ideal for model-testing purposes (owing to sporting clubs being active in coopetition activities, as well as other entrepreneurial behaviours), but it would be helpful to sample mainstream industries (in different countries) in the years to come. This will determine whether these results are transferrable to smaller-sized organisations in other populations.
3. The conceptual model was relatively simple, in terms of it having a series of linear paths. It would be useful to extend the conceptual model with more complex associations, like quadratic relationships and/or moderating effects. For instance, there might be environmental contingencies (e.g., hostility between industry rivals) that distort the respective relationships between these forms of coopetition and sales performance. In doing so, new evidence will emerge on whether there are boundaries to these statistical findings.
4. Although established, the scales were all from self-reported sources (shaped during the preliminary qualitative stage). In the future, academics could repeat this investigation using a mixture of survey-based operationalisations and archival measures. As a suggestion, sales performance could be captured through secondary data (albeit this is challenging to collect), whereas, constructs, such as coopetition, could be measured via existing survey-based approaches.

5. Different theoretical lenses and/or research designs may feature in future studies, and especially, to measure "how/why" issues in a longitudinal manner (subject to gaining access to data).

These limitations were not large concerns, but instead, offer ample opportunities for future research.

References

Ahn, J. D., Hong, S. D., & Park, Y. K. (2009). The historical and cultural identity of Taekwondo as a traditional Korean martial art. *International Journal of the History of Sport, 26*(11), 1716–1734.

Armstrong, J. S., & Overton, T. S. (1977). Estimating non-response bias in mail surveys. *Journal of Marketing Research, 14*(3), 396–402.

Barney, J. B. (1991). Firm resources and sustained competitive advantage. *Journal of Management, 17*(1), 99–120.

Barney, J. B. (2001). Is the resource-based "view" a useful perspective for strategic management research? Yes. *Academy of Management Review, 26*(1), 41–56.

Barney, J. B. (2018). Why resource-based theory's model of profit appropriation must incorporate a stakeholder perspective. *Strategic Management Journal, 39*(13), 3305–3325.

Barney, J. B., Ketchen, D. J., Jr., & Wright, M. (2011). The future of resource-based theory: Revitalization or decline? *Journal of Management, 37*(5), 1299–1315.

Bengtsson, M., & Kock, S. (2000). Coopetition in business networks: To cooperate and compete simultaneously. *Industrial Marketing Management, 29*(5), 411–426.

Bengtsson, M., & Kock, S. (2014). Coopetition - quo vadis? Past accomplishments and future challenges. *Industrial Marketing Management, 43*(2), 180–188.

Bouncken, R. B., & Kraus, S. (2013). Innovation in knowledge-intensive industries: The double-edged sword of coopetition. *Journal of Business Research, 66*(10), 2060–2070.

Bouncken, R. B., Fredrich, V., Ritala, P., & Kraus, S. (2018). Coopetition in new product development alliances: Advantages and tensions for incremental and radical innovation. *British Journal of Management, 29*(3), 391–410.

Bouncken, R. B., Gast, J., Kraus, S., & Bogers, M. (2015). Coopetition: A systematic review, synthesis, and future research directions. *Review of Managerial Science, 9*(3), 577–601.

Cadogan, J. W. (2012). International marketing, strategic orientations and business success: Reflections on the path ahead. *International Marketing Review, 29*(4), 340–348.

Cadogan, J. W., Kuivalainen, O., & Sundqvist, S. (2009). Export market-oriented behavior and export performance: Quadratic and moderating effects under differing degrees of market dynamism and internationalization. *Journal of International Marketing, 14*(4), 71–89.

Chaudhry, S., Crick, D., & Crick, J. M. (2019). Trade barriers and assistance requirements of South-Asian transnational entrepreneurs. In M. Y. Haddoud., P. Jones, and A.-K. E. Onjewu (Eds.), *International entrepreneurship in emerging markets: Nature, drivers, barriers and determinants* (pp. 115–140). Emerald.

Chetty, S. K., & Wilson, H. I. M. (2003). Collaborating with competitors to acquire resources. *International Business Review, 12*(1), 61–81.

Churchill, G. A., Jr. (1979). A paradigm for developing better measures of marketing constructs. *Journal of Marketing Research, 16*(1), 64–73.

Crick, D., & Crick, J. M. (2014). The internationalization strategies of rapidly internationalizing high-tech UK SMEs: Planned and unplanned activities. *European Business Review, 26*(5), 421–448.

Crick, D., & Crick, J. M. (2015). Learning and decision-making in marketing planning: A study of New Zealand vineyards. *Marketing Intelligence & Planning, 33*(5), 707–732.

Crick, D., & Crick, J. M. (2016a). Coopetition at the sports marketing/entrepreneurship interface: A case study of a Taekwondo organisation. *Marketing Intelligence & Planning, 34*(2), 169–187.

Crick, D., & Crick, J. M. (2016b). The first export order: A marketing innovation revisited. *Journal of Strategic Marketing, 24*(2), 77–89.

Crick, D., Chaudhry, S., & Crick, J. M. (2016). Trading in a competitive environment: South-Asian restaurants in the UK. *Strategic Change, 25*(4), 371–382.

Crick, D., Chaudhry, S., & Crick, J. M. (2018). Risks/rewards and an evolving business model: A case study of a small lifestyle business in the UK tourism sector. *Qualitative Market Research: An International Journal, 21*(2), 143–165.

Crick, J. M. (2015). Bridging the gap between threshold and dynamic capabilities: a qualitative study of the collaboration strategies of New Zealand wineries. unpublished Master of Business Studies thesis in management, Massey University.

Crick, J. M. (2018a). The facets, antecedents and consequences of coopetition: An entrepreneurial marketing perspective. *Qualitative Market Research: An International Journal, 21*(2), 253–272.

Crick, J. M. (2018b). Studying coopetition in a wine industry context: Directions for future research. *International Journal of Wine Business Research, 30*(3), 366–371.

Crick, J. M. (2018c). The antecedents and consequences of a customer value-oriented dominant logic: A dynamic managerial capabilities perspective. unpublished Doctor of Philosophy thesis in marketing, Loughborough University.

Crick, J. M. (2019a). Moderators affecting the relationship between coopetition and company performance. *Journal of Business & Industrial Marketing, 34*(2), 518–531.

Crick, J. M. (2019b). Incorporating coopetition into the entrepreneurial marketing literature: Directions for future research. *Journal of Research in Marketing and Entrepreneurship, 21*(1), 19–36.

Crick, J. M. (2020). The dark-side of coopetition: When collaborating with competitors is harmful for company performance. *Journal of Business & Industrial Marketing, 35*(2), 318–337.

Crick, J. M. (2021a). The dimensionality of the market orientation construct. *Journal of Strategic Marketing, 29*(4), 281–300.

Crick, J. M. (2021b). Unpacking the relationship between a coopetition-oriented mind-set and coopetition-oriented behaviours. *Journal of Business & Industrial Marketing, 36*(3), 400–419.

Crick, J. M. (2021c). Does competitive aggressiveness negatively moderate the relationship between coopetition and customer satisfaction performance? *Journal of Strategic Marketing* (forthcoming).

Crick, J. M. (2021d). Don't run before you can walk! The importance of fostering threshold capabilities in securing market-level survival. *International Journal of Entrepreneurship and Small Business* (forthcoming).

Crick, J. M. (2021e). Qualitative research in marketing: what can academics do better? *Journal of Strategic Marketing* (forthcoming).

Crick, J. M., & Crick, D. (2016c). Developing entrepreneurial resilience in the UK tourism sector. *Strategic Change, 25*(3), 315–325.

Crick, J. M., & Crick, D. (2018). Angel investors' predictive and control funding criteria: The importance of evolving business models. *Journal of Research in Marketing and Entrepreneurship, 20*(1), 34–56.

Crick, J. M., & Crick, D. (2019). Developing and validating a multi-dimensional measure of coopetition. *Journal of Business & Industrial Marketing, 34*(4), 665–689.

Crick, J. M., & Crick, D. (2020). Coopetition and COVID-19: Collaborative business-to-business marketing strategies in a pandemic crisis. *Industrial Marketing Management, 88*(1), 206–213.

Crick, J. M., & Crick, D. (2021a). The Yin and Yang nature of coopetition activities: Non-linear effects and the moderating role of competitive intensity for internationalised firms. *International Marketing Review, 38*(4), 690–716.

Crick, J. M., & Crick, D. (2021b). Coopetition and sales performance: Evidence from non-mainstream sporting clubs. *International Journal of Entrepreneurial Behavior & Research, 27*(1), 123–147.

Crick, J. M., & Crick, D. (2021c). Coopetition as an entrepreneurial strategy: focus on the wine sector. In L.-P. Dana (Ed.), *World encyclopaedia of entrepreneurship* (pp. 26–39). Edward Elgar.

Crick, J. M., & Crick, D. (2021d). The dark-side of coopetition: Influences on the paradoxical forces of cooperativeness and competitiveness across product-market strategies. *Journal of Business Research, 122*(1), 226–240.

Crick, J. M., & Crick, D. (2021e). Internationalizing the coopetition construct: Quadratic effects on financial performance under different degrees of export intensity and an export geographical scope. *Journal of International Marketing, 29*(2), 62–80.

Crick, J. M., Crick, D., & Peixinho, J. M. (2021a). Does industry experience positively moderate the quadratic relationship between coopetition and financial performance? Evidence from the New Zealand wine sector. *International Journal of Entrepreneurship and Small Business* (forthcoming).

Crick, J. M., Crick, D., & Chaudhry, S. (2021b). The dark-side of coopetition: it's not what you say, but the way that you do it. *Journal of Strategic Marketing* (forthcoming).

Crick, J. M., Karami, M., & Crick, D. (2021c). The impact of the interaction between an entrepreneurial marketing orientation and coopetition on business performance. *International Journal of Entrepreneurial Behavior & Research, 27*(6), 1423–1447.

Crick, J. M., Crick, D., & Tebbett, N. (2020a). Competitor orientation and value co-creation in sustaining rural New Zealand wine producers. *Journal of Rural Studies, 73*(1), 122–134.

Crick, J. M., Crick, D., & Chaudhry, S. (2020b). Entrepreneurial marketing decision-making in rapidly internationalising and de-internationalising start-up firms. *Journal of Business Research, 113*(1), 158–167.

Dana, L.-P., & Dana, T. E. (2005). Expanding the scope of methodologies used in entrepreneurship research. *International Journal of Entrepreneurship and Small Business, 2*(1), 79–88.

Dana, L.-P., Granata, J., Lasch, F., & Carnaby, A. (2013). The evolution of co-opetition in the Waipara wine cluster of New Zealand. *Wine Economics and Policy, 2*(1), 42–49.

Enders, C. K. (2003). Using the expectation maximization algorithm to estimate coefficient alpha for scales with item-level missing data. *Psychological Methods, 8*(3), 322–337.

Fabrigar, L. R., Wegener, D. T., MacCallum, R. C., & Strahan, E. J. (1999). Evaluating the use of exploratory factor analysis in psychological research. *Psychological Methods, 4*(3), 272–299.

Farrell, A. M., & Rudd, J. M. (2009). Factor analysis and discriminant validity: a brief review of some practical issues. In *Proceedings of the Australia and New Zealand Marketing Academy Conference.*

Felzensztein, C., & Deans, K. R. (2013). Marketing practices in wine clusters: Insights from Chile. *Journal of Business & Industrial Marketing, 28*(4), 357–367.

Felzensztein, C., Deans, K. R., & Dana, L.-P. (2019). Small firms in regional clusters: Local networks and internationalization in the Southern Hemisphere. *Journal of Small Business Management, 57*(2), 496–516.

Felzensztein, C., Gimmon, E., & Deans, K. R. (2018). Coopetition in regional clusters: Keep calm and expect unexpected changes. *Industrial Marketing Management, 69*(1), 116–124.

Felzensztein, C., Huemer, L., & Gimmon, E. (2010). The effects of co-location on marketing externalities in the salmon-farming industry. *Journal of Business & Industrial Marketing, 25*(1), 73–82.

Felzensztein, C., Stringer, C., Benson-Rea, M., & Freeman, S. (2014). International marketing strategies in industrial clusters: Insights from the Southern Hemisphere. *Journal of Business Research, 67*(5), 837–846.

Gallagher, D., & Mitchell, R. (2016). Complementary competition & cooperation: Developing coopetition as the antidote to sports marketing myopia in small sports clubs. In *North American Society of Sport Management Conference.*

Geldes, C., Heredia, J., Felzensztein, C., & Mora, M. (2017). Proximity as determinant of business cooperation for technological and non-technological innovations: A study of an agribusiness cluster. *Journal of Business & Industrial Marketing, 32*(1), 167–178.

Gnyawali, D. R., & Charleton, T. R. (2018). Nuances in the interplay of competition and cooperation: Towards a theory of coopetition. *Journal of Management, 44*(7), 2511–2534.

Gnyawali, D. R., & Park, B. J. R. (2011). Coopetition between giants: Collaboration with competitors for technological innovation. *Research Policy, 40*(5), 650–663.

Granata, J., Lasch, F., Le Roy, F., & Dana, L.-P. (2018). How do micro-firms manage coopetition? A study of the wine sector in France. *International Small Business Journal, 36*(3), 331–355.

Hamzah, M. I., Crick, J. M., Crick, D., Ali, S. A. M., & Yunus, N. M. (2021). The nature of the relationship between an entrepreneurial marketing orientation small business growth: evidence from Malaysia. *International Journal of Entrepreneurship and Small Business* (forthcoming).

Hansen, D. J., Deacon, J. H., Pascal, V. J., & Sethna, Z. (2020). The future is in the past: A framework for the marketing-entrepreneurship interface (MEI). *Journal of Business Research, 113*(1), 198–208.

Hills, G. E., Hultman, C. M., & Miles, M. P. (2008). The evolution and development of entrepreneurial marketing. *Journal of Small Business Management, 46*(1), 99–112.

Hodgkinson, I. R., Hughes, P., & Hughes, M. (2012). Re-examining the deployment of market orientation in the public leisure sector. *Journal of Marketing Management, 28*(11/12), 1249–1269.

Hoffmann, W., Lavie, D., Reuer, J. J., & Shiplov, A. (2018). The interplay of competition and cooperation. *Strategic Management Journal, 39*(12), 3033–3052.

Hong, E. (2011). Elite sport and nation-building in South Korea: South Korea as the dark horse in global elite sport. *International Journal of the History of Sport, 28*(7), 977–989.

Hunt, S. D., Sparkman, R. D., Jr., & Wilcox, J. B. (1982). The pre-test in survey research: Issues and preliminary findings. *Journal of Marketing Research, 19*(2), 269–273.

Jones, P., Ratten, V., & Hayduk, T. (2020). Sport, fitness, and lifestyle entrepreneurship. *International Entrepreneurship and Management Journal, 16*(3), 783–793.

Jones, P., Ratten, V., Klapper, R., & Fayolle, A. (2019). Entrepreneurial identity and context: Current trends and an agenda for future research. *International Journal of Entrepreneurship and Innovation, 20*(1), 3–7.

Jones, R., & Rowley, J. (2011). Entrepreneurial marketing in small businesses: A conceptual exploration. *International Small Business Journal, 29*(1), 25–36.

Kock, S., Nisuls, J., & Soderqvist, A. (2010). Coopetition: A source of international opportunities in Finnish SMEs. *Competitiveness Review: An International Business Journal, 20*(2), 111–125.

Lindell, M. K., & Whitney, D. J. (2001). Accounting for common method variance in cross-sectional research designs. *Journal of Applied Psychology, 86*(1), 114–121.

Lopez-Carril, S., Escamilla-Fajardo, P., Gonzalez-Serrano, M. H., Ratten, V., & Gonzalez-Garcia, R. J. (2020). The rise of social media in sport: A bibliometric analysis. *International Journal of Innovation and Technology Management, 17*(6), 1–29.

Lorgnier, N., & Su, C. J. (2014). Considering coopetition strategies in sport tourism networks: A look at the non-profit nautical sports clubs on the northern coast of France. *European Sport Management Quarterly, 14*(1), 87–109.

Luo, X., Slotegraaf, R. J., & Pan, X. (2006). Cross-functional coopetition: The simultaneous role of cooperation and competition within firms. *Journal of Marketing, 70*(2), 67–80.

Merkel, U. (2008). The politics of sport diplomacy and reunification in divided Korea: One nation, two countries and three flags. *International Review for the Sociology of Sport, 43*(3), 289–311.

Miragaia, D. A. M., Da Costa, C. D. M., & Ratten, V. (2018). Sport events at the community level: A pedagogical tool to improve skills for students and teachers. *Education and Training, 60*(5), 431–442.

Morgan, N. A., Vorhies, D. W., & Mason, C. H. (2009). Market orientation, marketing capabilities, and firm performance. *Strategic Management Journal, 30*(8), 909–920.

Morgan, T., Anokhin, S., Kretinin, A., & Frishammar, J. (2015). The dark-side of the entrepreneurial orientation and market orientation interplay: A new product development perspective. *International Small Business Journal, 33*(7), 731–751.

Morris, M. H., Schindehutte, M., & LaForge, R. W. (2002). Entrepreneurial marketing: A construct for integrating emerging entrepreneurship and marketing perspectives. *Journal of Marketing Theory and Practice, 10*(4), 1–19.

Newby, R., Watson, J., & Woodliff, D. (2003). SME survey methodology: Response rates, data quality, and cost effectiveness. *Entrepreneurship Theory and Practice, 28*(2), 163–172.

Peter, J. P. (1981). Construct validity: A review of basic issues and marketing practices. *Journal of Marketing Research, 18*(2), 133–145.

Peterson, R. A. (2000). A meta-analysis of variance accounted for and factor loadings in exploratory factor analysis. *Marketing Letters, 11*(3), 261–275.

Podsakoff, P. M., Mackenzie, S. B., Lee, J. Y., & Podsakoff, N. P. (2003). Common method biases in behavioral research: A critical review of the literature and recommended remedies. *Journal of Applied Psychology, 88*(5), 879–903.

Priem, R. L., & Butler, J. E. (2001). Is the resource-based view a useful perspective for strategic management research? *Academy of Management Review, 26*(1), 22–40.

Ranganathan, R., Ghosh, A., & Rosenkopf, L. (2018). Competition – Cooperation interplay during multi-firm technology coordination: The effect of firm heterogeneity on conflict and consensus in a technology standards organization. *Strategic Management Journal, 39*(12), 3193–3221.

Ratten, V. (2009). The impact of sports on team performance management. *Team Performance Management, 15*(3/4), 97–99.

Ratten, V. (2011a). International sports management: Current trends and future developments. *Thunderbird International Business Review, 53*(6), 679–686.

Ratten, V. (2011b). Sport-based entrepreneurship: Towards a new theory of entrepreneurship and sport management. *International Entrepreneurship and Management Journal, 7*(1), 57–69.

Ratten, V. (2012). Guest editor's introduction: Sports entrepreneurship: Towards a conceptualisation. *International Journal of Entrepreneurial Venturing, 4*(1), 1–17.

Ratten, V. (2014). Encouraging collaborative entrepreneurship in developing countries: The current challenges and a research agenda. *Journal of Entrepreneurship in Emerging Economies, 6*(3), 298–308.

Ratten, V. (2015). Athletes as entrepreneurs: The role of social capital and leadership ability. *International Journal of Entrepreneurship and Small Business, 25*(4), 442–455.

Ratten, V. (2016). The dynamics of sport marketing. *Marketing Intelligence & Planning, 34*(2), 162–168.

Ratten, V. (2017). Entrepreneurial sport policy. *International Journal of Sport Policy and Politics, 9*(4), 641–648.

Ratten, V. (2019). Sport entrepreneurship and public policy: Future trends and research developments. *Journal of Entrepreneurship and Public Policy, 8*(1), 207–216.

Ratten, V. (2020a). Sport technology: A commentary. *Journal of High Technology Management Research, 31*(1), 1–6.

Ratten, V. (2020b). Coronavirus disease (COVID-19) and sport entrepreneurship. *International Journal of Entrepreneurial Behavior & Research, 26*(6), 1379–1388.

Ratten, V. (2021), "Family business and sport entrepreneurship", *Journal of Family Business Management* (forthcoming).

Ratten, V., & Babiak, K. (2010). The role of social responsibility, philanthropy and entrepreneurship in the sport industry. *Journal of Management & Organization, 16*(4), 482–487.

Ratten, V., & Dickson, G. (2021). Disruptions in sport management from COVID-19: Lessons from entrepreneurship and innovation. In V. Ratten (Ed.), *Innovation and entrepreneurship in sport management* (pp. 9–21). Edward Elgar.

Ratten, V., & Ferreira, J. (2017). Entrepreneurship, innovation and sport policy: Implications for future research. *International Journal of Sport Policy and Politics, 9*(4), 575–577.

Ratten, V., & Jones, P. (2018). Future research directions for sport education: Toward an entrepreneurial learning approach. *Education and Training, 60*(5), 490–499.

Ratten, V., & Jones, P. (2020). New challenges in sport entrepreneurship for value creation. *International Entrepreneurship and Management Journal, 16*(3), 961–980.

Ratten, V., & Li, A. (2021). Coronavirus and sport crisis management: A knowledge spill-over perspective. In V. Ratten (Ed.). *Innovation and entrepreneurship in sport management* (pp. 159–167). Edward Elgar.

Ratten, V., & Nanere, M. (2020). Sport entrepreneurship and entrepreneurial ecosystems. In V. Ratten (Ed.), *Sport entrepreneurship: An economic, social and sustainability perspective* (pp. 75–92). Emerald.

Ratten, V., & Ratten, H. (2011). International sport marketing: Practical and future research implications. *Journal of Business & Industrial Marketing, 26*(8), 614–620.

Ratten, V., & Tajeddini, K. (2019). Entrepreneurship and sport business research: Synthesis and lessons: Introduction to the special journal issue. *International Journal of Sport Management and Marketing, 19*(1/2), 1–7.

Ratten, V., & Thompson, A.-J. (2020). Digital sport entrepreneurial ecosystems. *Thunderbird International Business Review, 62*(5), 565–578.

Ritala, P. (2012). Coopetition strategy – When is it successful? Empirical evidence on innovation and market performance. *British Journal of Management, 23*(3), 307–324.

Ritala, P., Golnam, A., & Wegmann, A. (2014). Coopetition-based business models: The case of Amazon.com. *Industrial Marketing Management, 43*(2), 236–249.

Rusko, R. (2011). Exploring the concept of coopetition: A typology for the strategic moves of the Finnish forest industry. *Industrial Marketing Management, 40*(2), 311–320.

Shu, C., Jin, J. L., & Zhou, K. Z. (2017). A contingent view of partner coopetition in international joint ventures. *Journal of International Marketing, 25*(3), 42–60.

Sraha, G., Sharma, R. R., Crick, D., & Crick, J. M. (2020). International experience, export commitment, distribution adaptation, and performance: A study of Ghanaian firms in B2B export markets. *Journal of Business & Industrial Marketing, 35*(11), 1715–1738.

Stewart, D. W. (1981). The application and misapplication of factor analysis in marketing research. *Journal of Marketing Research, 18*(1), 51–62.

Strese, S., Meuer, M. W., Flatten, T. C., & Brettel, M. (2016). Examining cross-functional coopetition as a driver of organizational ambidexterity. *Industrial Marketing Management, 57*(1), 40–52.

Suddaby, R. (2006). From the editors: What grounded theory is not. *Academy of Management Journal, 49*(4), 633–642.

Telfer, D. J. (2001). Strategic alliances along the Niagara wine route. *Tourism Management, 22*(1), 21–30.

Thukral, E., & Ratten, V. (2021). Sport innovation, entrepreneurship and digital ecosystems. In V. Ratten (Ed.), *Innovation and entrepreneurship in sport management* (pp. 122–136). Edward Elgar.

Vorhies, D. W., & Morgan, N. A. (2005). Benchmarking marketing capabilities for sustainable competitive advantage. *Journal of Marketing, 69*(1), 80–94.
Vorhies, D. W., Orr, L. M., & Bush, V. D. (2011). Improving customer-focused marketing capabilities and firm financial performance via marketing exploration and exploitation. *Journal of the Academy of Marketing Science, 39*(5), 736–756.
Wemmer, F., Emrich, E., & Koenigstorfer, J. (2016). The impact of coopetition-based open innovation on performance in non-profit sports clubs. *European Sport Management Quarterly, 16*(3), 341–363.
Zollo, M., & Winter, S. G. (2002). Deliberate learning and the evolution of dynamic capabilities. *Organization Science, 13*(3), 339–351.

CHAPTER 5

Australian Entrepreneurial Universities

Vanessa Ratten

Introduction

Australian universities are known globally for their high level of teaching, research and service activities. Despite being a small country in terms of population, Australian universities rank highly on most global university indexes. Despite the quality reputation of Australian universities, there are economic and social factors forcing the Australian education system to become more entrepreneurial by increasing the amount of partnerships occurring between public and private entities and by emphasising innovation and creativity in courses. This means the contribution of entrepreneurship education to the Australian economy cannot be downplayed or ignored (Foo, 2011). Leaders, teachers and students of educational institutions are increasingly acknowledging the importance of entrepreneurship in society (Jones et al., 2017). Realising the role education plays in society, the Australian government actively encourages entrepreneurship education (Ratten et al., 2019).

V. Ratten (✉)
La Trobe University, Melbourne, VIC, Australia
e-mail: v.ratten@latrobe.edu.au

V. Ratten (ed.), *Oceania Entrepreneurship*,
https://doi.org/10.1007/978-981-16-7341-2_5

Following the lead of other countries, Australia has adopted entrepreneurship education in the education system. The main goal of entrepreneurship education in a higher education context is to enable a student to create their own business. This means bridging the gap between education and practice to ensure a smooth transition for students once they have graduated to the marketplace. Entrepreneurship education also teaches broader skills such as communication and developing a business plan that is valued in society. In order to stay relevant and up to date with societal needs, entrepreneurship education has been introduced into the curriculum of most Australian universities.

Australia is facing a number of structural challenges that impact socio-economic growth. As a result, there has been a need to create self-employment opportunities and new skills that are relevant in the digital age. One of the most significant challenges is the increase in number of youths seeking employment. To alleviate these problems, entrepreneurship education is being prioritised. In addition, there is an emerging consensus that education should also incorporate societal benefits. More universities are requiring all students to have some form of entrepreneurship education. To do this training, time and resources are invested in entrepreneurship.

The rapid development of Australia has led to more focus on the growing competitiveness and expansion of firms from the country. As a result, the concept of an entrepreneurial university is being promoted as it creates a culture conducive to innovation in all aspects of behaviour including service, teaching and research. Despite the existence of entrepreneurial universities in Australia, there is a lack of studies on Australia which means what we know so far is limited. Therefore, a comprehensive understanding of Australian entrepreneurial universities is required. This will enrich the general entrepreneurship field by taking into account a more objective view of entrepreneurship. Therefore, it is important to ask: What is the current state of knowledge on Australian entrepreneurial universities and entrepreneurship education and where do we go from here?

Entrepreneurial Universities

Universities typically have three main missions: teaching, research and service but an entrepreneurial university goes further by emphasising the role of stakeholders in the university environment. In order to increase the level of entrepreneurship occurring in Australian society, the government is emphasising the role of education. The role of education in the economy has changed considerably over time due to increased acknowledgement about the link between entrepreneurial activity and knowledge management (Inkizhinov et al., 2021). Stolze (2021, p. 14) defines an entrepreneurial university as "an institution that explored new sources of funds, like patents, research contracts and industry partnerships". This means that in the past a university was focused just on teaching and research activities but due to the needs of the knowledge and service economy they have had to become more entrepreneurial in nature. This means thinking about new revenue and outreach activities that can occur through industry engagement. By integrating stakeholder needs from various sectors of the economy an entrepreneurial university can be more proactive and futuristic in thinking. Zhou and Peng (2008, p. 637) state that an entrepreneurial university is "the university that strongly influences the regional development of industries, as well as economic growth through high-tech entrepreneurship based on strong research, technology transfer and entrepreneurship capability". This means the distinguishing feature of an entrepreneurial university is how they are engaged in community activity.

Clark (1998) proposed that an entrepreneurial university is characterised by five main elements: (1) decision-making style, (2) organisational structure, (3) diversified funding base, (4) stimulated environment and (5) culture. The decision-making process refers to a more flexible model that is based on environmental conditions. This enables decisions to be made based on changing circumstances that might affect demand for certain courses. Thereby allowing for a more independent process that is decentralised. The organisational structure refers to the existence of research institutions, teaching facilities and science parks (Ratten, 2009). This mix of public and private entities allows for more potential collaboration. The diversified funding base enables a reduced reliance on government funding and more emphasis on alternative funding sources. This incentivises commercialisation of knowledge through partnerships. The stimulated environment refers to staff in the university being motivated to pursue new tasks. This enables the generation of new ideas that lead to entrepreneurial ventures (Feranita et al., 2017). Culture refers to the style of working that encourages innovation, risk-taking and futuristic thinking.

Knowledge that is created at universities can be spilled over to other sectors of the economy through knowledge transfer (Guerrero et al., 2016). Universities are increasingly being tasked with the role of connecting different stakeholders in society. In order to function in an entrepreneurial way, universities need to focus on time issues (Aguinis & Bakker, 2021). This occurs through knowledge transfer aimed at contributing to the broader development of society. Stakeholders of universities include citizens, students, alumni, the community and businesses who each contribute to the exchange of knowledge. Due to the growth in the knowledge economy and increased emphasis on digitalisation, universities are being viewed in an entrepreneurial manner. This enables them to pursue additional social or knowledge missions in conjunction with their traditional teaching and research roles. Moreover, lower levels of government funding have resulted in universities needing to diversify their income sources. As a consequence, universities are focusing on how to contribute to both social and economic objectives through entrepreneurial behaviour.

Benneworth (2007) suggested that there are four main paths that universities can pursue in their transformation into entrepreneurial entities: naïve, growth, consolidation and reach out. Naïve means that they are becoming more involved in entrepreneurship through unplanned activities. Growth refers to a focus on entrepreneurship as a way to build an income. Consolidation means focusing on cost savings whilst reach out refers to actively engaging with others on entrepreneurial projects. Knowledge transfer in a university setting involves converting and transferring information into useable outcomes. This includes commercialising basic research that can then be used in other societal contexts (Obeidat et al., 2016). Universities play a key role in supporting innovation and facilitating economic development. They have done this by transforming into more accountable institutions that take pride in facilitating community interaction (Ratten, 2017). The notion of universities being entrepreneurial is not new as some have incorporated innovation into their activities for a long time period. However, referring to universities as entrepreneurial universities is a relatively new term that has corresponded with the interest in entrepreneurship.

Australian Universities

There are 42 universities in Australia most of which are public universities funded by the government but also some newer private universities. The private universities include Bond University, Carnegie Mellon University (Australia campus), Torrens University and the University of Notre Dame. The group of eight universities in Australia refer to research-intensive universities. These include the University of Adelaide, Australian National University, the University of Melbourne, Monash University, University of New South Wales and the University of Sydney. The group of eight universities are the oldest and largest universities in Australia. Six of the group of eight are ranked in the world's top 100 universities. In addition, more than a quarter of all higher education students in Australia attend a group of eight universities. A majority of the research funding from the government and industry goes to the group of eight universities. The group of eight are also referred to as the sandstone universities. Table 5.1 states the name, year of establishment, city and state of the group of eight universities in Australia.

The innovative research universities group comprises seven universities: Charles Darwin University, James Cook University, Griffith University, La Trobe University, Flinders University, Murdoch University and Western

Table 5.1 Australian group of eight members

Name	*Year of establishment*	*City*	*State*
University of Adelaide	1874	Adelaide	South Australia
Australian National University	1946	Canberra	Australian Captial Territory
University of Sydney	1850	Sydney	New South Wales
University of Melbourne	1853	Melbourne	Victoria
University of New South Wales	1949	Sydney	New South Wales
University of Queensland	1909	Brisbane	Queensland
Monash University	1958	Melbourne	Victoria
University of Western Australia	1966	Perth	Western Australia

Source Author's own

Sydney University. These universities are younger universities that were established in the 1960s and 1970s. They focus more on innovation in educational delivery and design. Therefore, they are considered more teaching-focused than the research-focused group of eight universities. Table 5.2 states the name, year of establishment, city and state of the innovative research universities.

The Australian Technology Network is a group of five universities: Curtin University, RMIT University, University of South Australia, University of Technology Sydney and Deakin University. Originally the Queensland University of Technology was part of the group but left in 2018. The universities in the group have more of a focus on industry engagement. Most of the universities in this group were originally institutes of technology that changed their names to universities. Each of these universities has its main campus in the central business district of their state's capital city. The universities focus on applied research, which is why they are called a technology group. Table 5.3 states the name, year of establishment, year of university status, city and state for the Australian Technology Network of Universities.

The regional universities network is a group of seven universities that have their main campus in regional areas. They include Charles

Table 5.2 Innovative research universities

Name	*Year of establishment*	*City*	*State*
Charles Darwin University	2003	Darwin	Northern Territory
James Cook University	1961	Cairns	Queensland
Griffith University	1971	Brisbane	Queensland
La Trobe University	1964	Melbourne	Victoria
Flinders University	1966	Adelaide	South Australia
Murdoch University	1973	Perth	Western Australia
Western Sydney University	1989	Sydney	New South Wales

Source Author's own

Table 5.3 Australian Technology Network of Universities

Name	*Year of establishment*	*Year of university status*	*City*	*State*
Curtin University	1902	1986	Perth	Western Australia
RMIT University	1887	1992	Melbourne	Victoria
University of South Australia	1856	1991	Adelaide	South Australia
University of Technology Sydney	1964	1988	Sydney	New South Wales
Deakin University	1974	1974	Geelong	Victoria

Source Author's own

Sturt University, Central Queensland University, Federation University, Southern Cross University, University of New England, University of Southern Queensland and the University of the Sunshine Coast. These universities focus on regional areas but many also have large online courses and campuses in city regions. Table 5.4 states the name, year of establishment, university status, cities and state of the regional Australian universities.

Entrepreneurship Education

Australian universities have increasingly been engaged in entrepreneurial activities through education in order to increase their competitiveness. Entrepreneurs have greatly contributed to the economic growth of Australia by creating and managing new business ventures. An entrepreneur is an individual who is an effective risk-taker and is persistent in pursuing ideas. The current approach to entrepreneurship education emphasises creativity and problem-solving. This is due to the topic of entrepreneurship involving many different types of activities. Entrepreneurship by definition involves adapting to change based on market feedback. These skills are valued now more than ever due to the effects of the COVID-19 pandemic. More people are studying entrepreneurship with increased enrolments in both undergraduate and postgraduate courses.

Table 5.4 Regional Australian universities

Name	*Year of establishment*	*University status*	*Cities*	*State*
Charles Sturt University	1895	1989	Albury-Wodonga, Goulburn, Wagga Wagga	New South Wales
Central Queensland University	1967	1992	Bundaberg, Gladstone, Mackay, Rockhampton, Sydney, Brisbane	Queensland
Federation University	1870	1994	Ballarat, Ararat, Horsham, Stawell and Churchill	Victoria
Southern Cross University	1954	1994	Coffs Harbour, Lismore, Tweed Heads	New South Wales
University of New England	1938	1954	Armidale	New South Wales
University of Southern Queensland	1967	1992	Toowoomba, Springfield, Ipswich	Queensland
University of the Sunshine Coast	1994	1994	Sippy Downs, Hervey Bay, Caboolture, Gympie	Queensland

Source Author's own

The idea of entrepreneurship education has quickly been adopted by the Australian government as a way of encouraging regional development. The excitement around entrepreneurship has led to a situation where it is expected that students have entrepreneurial training. The concept of entrepreneurship education is often used metaphorically in terms of referring to any kind of education that embeds creativity and risk-taking activity. Countries are focusing more on higher education reforms in order to strategically plan for the future. This is due to there being a change in the autonomy and accountability of higher education institutions. This has resulted in an expectation that universities contribute to developing their entrepreneurial ecosystems. To do this universities need to transcend past expectations to include new developments including changing social and technological demands. This will help produce more human capital that can contribute to the growth of the knowledge economy.

Entrepreneurship as a field of study has its origins in the work of Cantillon (1755) who differentiated self-employed workers from employed workers. This means emphasising the way some people prefer autonomy and independence in their employment conditions. Initially first conceptualisations of entrepreneurship emphasised risk-taking under certain conditions. Nowadays, the entrepreneurship research field is amongst the most popular areas of general management studies. Kraus et al. (2011, p. 60) state that entrepreneurship is "the process of value creation through the identification and exploitation of opportunities eg by developing new products or by seeking new markets or both". In order to capitalise on market opportunities, entrepreneurs need to be able to access the appropriate resources.

Most entrepreneurship education courses are offered at the university level but increasingly new programmes are emerging at the primary and high school level. Education is on the political agenda in Australia as a way of increasing the living standards of citizens. As a result, entrepreneurial forms of education are emerging due to the way it bridges practice with theory. Whilst there is still ongoing debate about whether entrepreneurship can be taught, the general consensus is that it can.

Education about entrepreneurship involves teaching skills related to starting a new business. This involves providing individuals with the knowledge about how to recognise a market opportunity. There are also other skills taught in entrepreneurship classes including commercialisation, initiating a business venture and managing growth. A different learning environment is needed in order to study entrepreneurship. This is due to the topic of entrepreneurship involving the use of creative skills and inquisitiveness. Thus, the way entrepreneurship is taught often involves immersive or experiential learning. Entrepreneurship education as a teaching style emphasises problem-solving and thinking outside the box. This means it is action-orientated and more practically focused than other subject areas. In addition, project-based learning that mixes knowledge with practice is valued.

Entrepreneurship education has revolutionised existing teaching methods by encouraging more interactive involvement. There is more student demand for practical skills that have led to interest in entrepreneurship. In order to succeed in the fast-changing competitive business marketplace, students need to acquire relevant skills. Entrepreneurship education emphasises creativity and imagination in a business context. This means it incorporates the contemporary needs of society in a way that traditional subjects do not. Furthermore, entrepreneurship education mostly involves teaching students about how to start a business but has recently changed to incorporate other skills such as entrepreneurial leadership and thinking. This has meant that knowledge about how to obtain resources and then manage risks is taught.

Knowledge Transfer Activities

Knowledge is a critical resource in the global marketplace and provides a competitive advantage. In order to facilitate effective knowledge sharing, universities need to be involved in inter-organisational knowledge practices. To do this, more universities are focusing on partnerships as a way to acquire relevant information. Collaborative systems can be utilised to obtain knowledge that generates value. Universities are relying on external sources of knowledge obtained through collaboration for their innovation success. This means that inter-organisational partnerships provide sources of knowledge. Moreover, creating effective environments for sharing knowledge is important in the marketplace. To do this innovation ecosystems can be utilised as they enable a network of actors to develop for the specific purpose of sharing knowledge. Within an university innovation ecosystem there are two main types of knowledge that are transferred: explicit and tacit. Explicit knowledge is codified and can be easily transferred. Tacit knowledge is intangible and difficult to exchange.

Universities utilise a range of channels to transfer knowledge including through academic engagement and research commercialisation. Academic engagement refers to the collaborative activities academics are involved in that enable them to transfer knowledge. This can include consultancy, research and teaching activities. Research commercialisation refers to activities that enable knowledge to be used for business purposes. Typically, it involves financial gain that can be obtained from intellectual property. Examples include licensing, patenting and spin-off activities.

University knowledge transfer activities can be differentiated in terms of diversity and intensity. The diversity refers to the number and variety of different knowledge transfer activities. The quantity in terms of volume can result in more knowledge being transferred. However, some activities might result in more useful knowledge so the quality of knowledge transfer activities also needs to be considered. Some universities might prefer to focus on a small number of knowledge transfer activities in order to manage better the knowledge flow. This enables them to control the way knowledge is dispersed to others. As a consequence, universities might focus on a specific knowledge transfer strategy. This is a popular as way of stressing key university activities that are expected to result in high levels of knowledge being obtained. Normally these specific knowledge transfer activities are planned but they can also occur in an unplanned and sporadic way. This leads to knowledge being spilled over to others based on interaction.

The intensity of knowledge transfer refers to the quality and amount of knowledge being exchanged. Specific events might result in a high level of knowledge being obtained. Innovation is a process that unfolds over time and reactions to an innovation are time dependent. Time is a concept that can be hard to describe due to its malleable nature. This means whilst time normally refers to temporal aspects it can also be described based on individual perception. An important way to increase entrepreneurial behaviour is through education. Time has a linear duration that can be understood in different contexts. It is difficult to put into words what time is due to its elusive nature. This is due to time being based on cultural and social conditions that make it hard to define. This difficulty means that time can be misunderstood due to its multiple meanings.

Interaction in communities provides a useful way of connecting with others (Rheingold, 1993). This enables individuals to contribute to the innovation process in an easy way. Universities engage in the innovation process through creating and managing entrepreneurial teams. Schjoedt and Kraus (2009, p. 515) define an entrepreneurial team as "two or more persons who have an interest, both financial and otherwise, in, and commitment to a venture's future and success; whose work is interdependent in the pursuit of common goals and venture success; who are accountable to the entrepreneurial team and for the venture' who are considered to be at the executive level with executive responsibility in the early phases of the venture; including founding and pre-start-up; and who are seen as a social entity by themselves and by others". This lengthy definition acknowledges that there are different tasks involved in being part of an entrepreneurial team. In the initial stages of a startup the involvement might be around financing issues in other stages it can involve management functions (Kokkranikal & Morrison, 2011). The concept of a team means there is a sense of mutual dependence. This differs to a group, which consists of a number of people with separate interests (Ratten & Ferreira, 2017). Individuals in a team work together on a joint projects thereby implying collaboration. Robbins and Judge (2008, p. 123) define a group as "two or more individuals, interacting and interdependent, who have come together to achieve particularly objectives". A team can be distinguished from a group due to its members viewing themselves as a social unit (Schjoedt & Kraus, 2009). This means that members of a team have a commitment to achieving a certain outcome. This can include sharing information and helping each other with tasks.

Universities engage in a process of strategic entrepreneurship to manage their teams. This involves a university simultaneously focusing on new market opportunities whilst considering future plans. The emphasis is on obtaining a competitive advantage through identifying new opportunities that best match the firm's strategic direction. The sharing of knowledge also facilitates the way members of a team interact with each other (Palacios et al., 2008). By engaging with one another it shows a degree of commitment. An entrepreneurial team goes beyond normal team activities by embedding a sense of innovation and proactiveness in its actions (Ratten, 2011). In order to utilise the new business opportunities derived from entrepreneurship education, a more profound understanding of it needs to be developed. This can be done by analysing the entrepreneurial ecosystem literature (Ratten, 2014).

Entrepreneurial Ecosystems

The way entrepreneurial ecosystems are defined is a work in progress. This is due to the field still being developed and there being concurrent work on innovation ecosystems. Entrepreneurial ecosystem emphasises the role of the economic and social environment in influencing entrepreneurial behaviour. This means context plays an important role in either fostering or hindering entrepreneurship. Contexts that are favourable for entrepreneurship utilise social relationships in order to facilitate entrepreneurial action. Thereby enabling synergies to develop amongst members of an entrepreneurial ecosystem. An entrepreneurial ecosystem functions in a fluid way developing based on market conditions. This means there is a degree of uncertainty as to how the market will progress. This uncertainty enables flexibility to be used in a universities market relationships. In addition, there are location-specific characteristics that exist in an universities entrepreneurial ecosystem making it difficult to copy.

Within an universities entrepreneurial ecosystem entities learn through continuous and active engagement. This enables information to be disseminated in a way that leads to conducive learning. Part of being in an entrepreneurial ecosystem requires some form of experimentation. This helps members to try new paths and if needed reconfigure business practices. In a certain environment, different entities including businesses, citizens and public agencies work together on a university's entrepreneurial projects. Each member of an entrepreneurial ecosystem contributes in their own way to its development. Each entity is thereby affected by the continual changes that occur. However, the health of an entrepreneurial ecosystem depends on the inputs of its members.

Contexts that have greater opportunities to obtain knowledge are normally more entrepreneurial. Knowledge is obtained in various ways in an ecosystem environment. This includes through direct or indirect communication with other members. The creation of new university partnerships often requires specific forms of knowledge. This usually means the knowledge is obtained in direct ways with a purpose in mind. In addition, the commercialisation of ideas enables knowledge to be dispersed in an environment. To understand this process, ecological systems theory can be used. This theory suggests that "individuals are embedded within environments with which they interact to influence development" (Roosa et al., 2009, p. 328). This means individuals interact with others in their university environment based on need. As a result, individuals construct beliefs about their university environment that influence their behaviour. The basis of ecological system theory discusses how individuals are nested within four main systems: the microsystem, mesosystem, exosystem and macrosystem (Bronfenbrenner, 1979). The microsystem concerns the direct experiences and interactions an individual has in their environment. The mesosystem involves social interactions in the environment. The exosystem includes community settings that influence individual behaviour. The macrosystem involves the cultural influences or ideologies an individual acquires in their environment.

An individual in a universities ecosystem can be the main source of knowledge. Knowledge is also influenced by the market conditions and local specifics. Knowledge spillovers can be defined as shared information of value. This means unlike information that is considered general and easy to obtain, knowledge goes a step further in providing valuable outcomes. Entrepreneurship is a combination of persistence and circumstance. The persistence is evident in the ability of an entrepreneur to continue despite headship. For some entrepreneurs, they need to overcome market obstacles as they progress in the marketplace. This involves thinking in a strategic way about what steps they need to take in order to make their idea a reality. The circumstance involves the broader context in which a business operates. Universities are embedded in the social environment due to the need to manage relationships. This means that they interact with others in order to derive certain outcomes. In order to understand the interactions that occur it is helpful to focus on how universities evaluate these market opportunities. An ecosystem enables entities within a given environment to connect and interact. This is helpful in producing certain outcomes that are based on entrepreneurial needs. Ecosystems consist of a group of entities who connect based on mutual gain. This set of interdependent actors facilitates productive entrepreneurship.

Entrepreneurship can be a challenging psychological endeavour as there are multiple tasks to manage. This means entrepreneurs need to balance different objectives in order to obtain a certain result. The negative impact of setbacks can be difficult for an entrepreneur. This means they need to be resilient and proactive about solving potential problems. Entrepreneurs need to identify business opportunities then be able to mobilise their resources. This task can be difficult depending on the business context. In highly competitive environments, entrepreneurs need to engage in an idiosyncratic set of activities. Social networks can help an entrepreneur develop business opportunities. The resources and knowledge arising from a social network can help speed up the entrepreneurship process. Well-connected entrepreneurs are able to utilise their personal networks as a source of competitive advantage. Social networks are a source of emotional support to entrepreneurs. This enables them to obtain advice on how to react in the marketplace.

Entrepreneurs can utilise their social network to obtain help from well-connected individuals. This can include endorsements about the viability of a new project. Thereby an entrepreneur's social network provides a valuable source of support. The quality and nature of an entrepreneur's social network can impact their outcomes. This is due to some relationships being more beneficial than others. In addition, the strength of network ties can relate to the amount of information exchanged. Strong network ties facilitate the sharing of frequent amounts of information. This can be helpful in determining the direction of market changes. As a result, strong network ties generally result in high levels of social support. This includes a sense of solidarity amongst network members. An outcome of this is more reciprocity amongst social network members in the way information is shared. By focusing on the needs of individual network members then the kind of information given can be more strategic. Such close collaboration enables trust to develop in terms of how information is utilised. This can facilitate timely sharing of information that is valuable. Individuals obtain knowledge, skills and experience through education. This can lead to more productive individuals that contribute to societal well-being.

Entrepreneurial ecosystems provide a relational way that individuals can interact with others in their environment. This means that the environment is not stagnant but rather is fluid and constantly evolving. The main components of an ecosystem include access to capital, labour and services; engagement with others and government policy direction. In addition, the attitudes individuals and entities have towards entrepreneurship influences the success of an ecosystem. Local cultural attitudes play a key role in assessing whether entrepreneurship is a good or bad activity.

Entrepreneurial ecosystems can be understood from a regional planning and economic perspective. This is due to the way a place impacts the level of entrepreneurial behaviour in a university. The regional planning literature has focused on place as being a key indicator of economic growth. This has led to an emphasis on economic geography as a way of understanding the university context. An entrepreneurial ecosystem provides a way of understanding how individuals are actively engaged in their environment. This means it is built on regional innovation systems thinking but emphasises entrepreneurship.

Entrepreneurial Innovation Systems

The current research entrepreneurship education stands to benefit from new insights from the Australian context. This involves crafting new research specifically related to the culture and society existing in Australia. The concept of innovation ecosystems normally has a business focus. This is due to the way innovation influences business decisions. The term innovation ecosystem is derived from the pre-existing literature on business environments. Adner (2006, p. 2) defined an innovation ecosystem as "the collaborative arrangements through which firms combine their individual offerings into a coherent, customer-facing solution". Within this definition there is an emphasis on the interaction that occurs between a firm and its customers in the market environment. This means there is some kind of collaboration that occurs that acknowledges the importance of the interaction. Many researchers use the term innovation ecosystem as a general concept and do not specify its meaning. This lack of coherence around its meaning can make it hard to understand. The innovation component of innovation ecosystems refers to positive change. This normally involves some kind of ingenuity in the form of idea generation. Innovation can have different connotations depending on the context but normally it applies to a business setting.

Innovation ecosystems are a useful metaphor to describe how innovation is shared and used within a certain context. This means it is a distinctive field of research that provides a way of understanding change in the marketplace. The concept can be ambiguous in meaning due to the variety of ways it can be interpreted. Despite the widespread use of the term there is still some hesitation in fully understanding its meaning in a university context. Therefore, it is useful to also consider the type of university and its impact on innovation ecosystems. The system component of an innovation ecosystem implies that there is some degree of organisation. This means that entities within an ecosystem acknowledge the role they play in developing an innovative environment. Moreover, the relationships amongst these entities evolve based on the systemic interactions that occur. These interactions can be planned and unplanned depending on their occurrence. Furthermore, the system can be best analysed in terms of its inputs and outputs that involve any form of innovation. Within a system inputs are transformed into outputs based on the market demand. The eco component of an innovation ecosystem refers to the ecological or natural environment. This term is useful in highlighting how the business environment is similar to the ecological world in terms of things growing, dying and changing. It is also useful in suggested that like the natural environment, there are different roles entities play in its evolution. For example, there are naturally strong and weak entities that are needed in an environment in order for it to function in a proper way.

Universities need to collaborate with others in order to develop a business idea. This has led to a need to be part of an innovation ecosystem, which is comprised of a number of firms relying on each other for innovation purposes. The interdependency existing in an innovation ecosystem can result in more value creation but can also place restrictions on member activity. This is due to the way firms might delay certain actions until other members of the ecosystem can fulfill their obligations. Thus, rather than acting in a purely individualistic way, an ecosystem requires firms to consider how their actions might affect others. Firms can utilise the interdependency to create synergies and network effects.

More innovations are being created through universities engaged in cross-industry and public/private partnerships. The cross-industry partnerships involve entities from different sectors collaborating on a project for a joint gain. This is needed for projects that try to create a new product to solve a social need. It also enables entities from various sectors to piggyback on university research and development efforts. This can be helpful in obtaining funding and support for projects that are resource intensive. There are a number of connected entities in an ecosystem that shape entrepreneurial activity. This involves individuals and entities exchanging information beyond the normal university, industry and sectoral boundaries.

Entrepreneurship is influenced by culture and society. In addition, location-based entities such as governments, investors and universities can facilitate entrepreneurial behaviour in universities. Leadership is needed in a place in order to make an entrepreneurial ecosystem successful. This is due to the coordination of resources requiring strategic action. In order to pursue entrepreneurship leaders need to induce others to perform certain actions. The networks of entities that exist in an ecosystem are not bound by contractual relationships. Rather they share common interests that are aimed at proactive behaviour. This requires university leaders to develop deliberate strategies. Support organisations such as accelerators, incubators and technology transfer offices can lead to innovative ecosystem development.

Conclusion

This chapter has focused on the role of entrepreneurial universities in Australia. The range of universities existing in Australia including the group of eight, technology network and regional universities was stated. This led to a discussion about the way entrepreneurship education is becoming embedded in Australian universities through a process of knowledge transfer. The role of entrepreneurial universities in Australian society was stated in terms of the development of entrepreneurial and innovative ecosystems. This meant that there needs to be more focus on the interlinkages between different entities within an Australian university environment in order to facilitate more public/private partnerships.

This will further increase technology transfer levels and lead to the development of more entrepreneurial behaviour.

References

Adner, R. (2006). Match your innovation strategy to your innovation ecosystem. *Harvard Business Review, 84*(4), 98.

Aguinis, H., & Bakker, R. M. (2021). Time is of the essence: Improving the conceptualization and measurement of time. *Human Resource Management Review, 31*(2), 100763.

Benneworth, P. (2007). Seven samurai opening up the ivory tower? The construction of Newcastle as an entrepreneurial university. *European Planning Studies, 15*(4), 487–509.

Bronfenbrenner, U. (1979). Contexts of child rearing: Problems and prospects. *American Psychologist, 34*(10), 844.

Cantillon, R. (1755). *Essai sur la nature de commerce en ge'ne'ral.* Macmillan (English translation: Higgs, H., 1931, for the Royal Economic Society).

Clark, B. (1998). *Creating entrepreneurial universities: Organizational pathways of transformation: Issues in higher education.* Elsevier.

Feranita, F., Kotlar, J., & De Massis, A. (2017). Collaborative innovation in family firms: Past research, current debates and agenda for future research. *Journal of Family Business Strategy, 8*, 137–156.

Foo, M. (2011). Emotions and entrepreneurial opportunity recognition. *Entrepreneurship Theory & Practice, March*, 375–393.

Guerrero, M., Urbano, D., Fayolle, A., Klofsten, M., & Mian, S. (2016). Entrepreneurial universities: Emerging models in the new social and economic landscape. *Small Business Economics, 47*(3), 551–563.

Inkizhinov, B., Gorenskaia, E., Nazarov, D., & Klarin, A. (2021). Entrepreneurship in emerging markets: Mapping the scholarship and suggesting future research directions. *International Journal of Emerging Markets, 16*(7), 1404–1429.

Jones, P., Jones, A., Williams-Burnett, N., & Ratten, V. (2017). Let's get physical: Stories of entrepreneurial activity from sports coaches/instructors. *The International Journal of Entrepreneurship and Innovation, 18*(4), 219–230.

Kokkranikal, J., & Morrison, A. (2011). Community networks and sustainable livelihoods in tourism: The role of entrepreneurial innovation. *Tourism Planning & Development, 8*(2), 137–156.

Kraus, S., Kauranen, I., & Reschke, C. H. (2011). Identification of domains for a new conceptual model of strategic entrepreneurship using the configuration approach. *Management Research Review, 34*(1), 58–74.

Obeidat, B., Al-Suradi, M., Masadeh, R., & Tarhini, A. (2016). The impact of knowledge management on innovation: An empirical study on Jordanian consultancy firms. *Management Research Review, 39*(10), 1214–1238.

Palacios, D., Gil, I., & Garrigos, F. (2008). The impact of knowledge management on innovation and entrepreneurship in the biotechnology and telecommunications industries. *Small Business Economics, 32*(3), 291–301.

Ratten, V. (2009). Adoption of technological innovations in the m-commerce industry. *International Journal of Technology Marketing, 4*(4), 355–367.

Ratten, V. (2011). Sport-based entrepreneurship: Towards a new theory of entrepreneurship and sport management. *International Entrepreneurship and Management Journal, 7*(1), 57–69.

Ratten, V. (2014). Future research directions for collective entrepreneurship in developing countries: A small and medium-sized enterprise perspective. *International Journal of Entrepreneurship and Small Business, 22*(2), 266–274.

Ratten, V. (2017). Entrepreneurial sport policy. *International Journal of Sport Policy and Politics, 9*(4), 641–648.

Ratten, V., Braga, V., Álvarez-García, J., & Del Río, M. D. L. C. (Eds.). (2019). *Tourism innovation: Technology*. Routledge.

Ratten, V., & Ferreira, J. J. (2017). Future research directions for cultural entrepreneurship and regional development. *International Journal of Entrepreneurship and Innovation Management, 21*(3), 163–169.

Rheingold, H. (1993). *The virtual community: Homesteading on the electronic frontier*. Addison Eesley.

Robbins, S. P., & Judge, J. A. (2008). *Essentials of organizational behavior*, Pearson.

Roosa, M. W., White, R. M., Zeiders, K. H., & Tein, J. Y. (2009). An examination of the role of perceptions in neighborhood research. *Journal of Community Psychology, 37*(3), 327–341.

Schjoedt, L., & Kraus, S. (2009). Entrepreneurial teams: Definition and performance factors. *Management Research News, 32*, 513–524.

Stolze, A. (2021). A meta-ethnography on HEIs' transformation into more entrepreneurial institutions: Towards an action-framework proposition. *Industry and Higher Education, 35*(1), 14–27.

Zhou, C., & Peng, X. (2008). The entrepreneurial university in China: Nonlinear paths. *Science and Public Policy, 35*(9), 637–646.

CHAPTER 6

Entrepreneurship in Australia: Social Values and Perceptions

Esha Thukral

Introduction

Entrepreneurship has been the driving force for job creation, economic growth, and competitiveness. It not only contributes to personal fulfilment but also the attainment of social objectives (Maritz, 2015). Entrepreneurship is essential for the overall growth of the nation. Thus, it is an essential part of the business dynamism in market economies. Although there is no single definition of entrepreneurship accepted by the research community, there is still a general unanimity that; entrepreneurship is the creation of something new. According to Professor Howard Stevenson, "entrepreneurship is the pursuit of opportunity beyond resources controlled" (Eisenmann, 2013). Entrepreneurship can be defined as a process of bringing together the necessary factors of production consisting of human, physical, and informational resources in an efficient manner to create new products or services or produce an

E. Thukral (✉)
La Trobe University, Melbourne, Australia
e-mail: T.esha@latrobe.edu.au

V. Ratten (ed.), *Oceania Entrepreneurship*,
https://doi.org/10.1007/978-981-16-7341-2_6

existing product at a competitive cost (Lazear, 2005). Both the definitions take into account the individual and the society within which the individual is embedded. Schumpeter too talked about the interaction between the individual and the environment (context) (Stevenson, 2000). Thus, the process of entrepreneurship is based on the "interaction between the individual, their intuition, society and culture" (Kirkley, 2016b, p. 293). Therefore, together with the individual, the study of the context (culture, beliefs), the ecosystem is also integral to truly understand entrepreneurship in a particular country or region.

Ease of Starting a Business: Entrepreneurial Ecosystem

Evidence from research and surveys suggests that Australia has a good entrepreneurial ecosystem. Similarly, Australia was awarded the fifth· position in Global Entrepreneurship Index (GEI) 2018, which measures the health of the entrepreneurial ecosystem in 137 countries (The Global Entrepreneurship and Development Institute, 2018). Global Entrepreneurship Monitor (GEM) report in 2019 ranked Australia as number ten for ease of starting a business against 50 economies globally (Moyle et al., 2020). According to a recent World Bank survey, "Doing Business 2020", Australia scored the 14th position in the world for the ease of doing business in 2020 (Tang, 2019). World Bank "Doing Business" survey assesses regulations across 190 countries in 12 business regulatory areas to evaluate the business environment in each country. This year ten out of the 12 indicators were used to evaluate the business environment. The study looks at rules and regulations; affecting a business since its inception, all through its operation stage to the wind-down stage, that is starting a business, dealing with construction permits, getting electricity, registering property, getting credit, protecting minority investor, paying taxes, trading across borders, enforcing contracts, and resolving insolvency (World Bank, 2019).

Economies that score a higher rank in the survey have a more conducive environment for the entrepreneurial activity to take place as "the knowledge that is relevant for entrepreneurial action is embedded in the ecosystem structures and requires individual-level action to extract it" (The Global Entrepreneurship and Development Institute, 2018). However, despite Australia being a very easy place to start a business, fewer entrepreneurs were found to be entering the market. Thus, the picture of Australia's entrepreneurial activity is mixed (Australian Government: Department of Industry, Science, Energy, Resources: Office of the Chief Economist, 2020).

The entrepreneurial framework conditions matter because they provide a regulatory environment in two aspects, firstly who decides to be an entrepreneur and secondly to what extent the new business ventures are able to attain their full potential. The first aspect is modulated mostly by soft framework conditions, such as social beliefs, norms, and cultural preferences, whereas the second aspect is modulated by a variety of entrepreneurial framework conditions, namely, research and development, government, infrastructure, financial sector, and corporate sector (The Global Entrepreneurship and Development Institute, 2018).

It is, therefore, evident that various forces shape the entrepreneurial environment as entrepreneurship does not take place or flourish in a vacuum. A mix of attitudes, resources, and infrastructure (also known as "entrepreneurial ecosystem") are needed to support entrepreneurship or entrepreneurial activity. A vibrant ecosystem supports innovation and new venture creation. The prime attributes of the vibrant ecosystem are "deep reservoirs of early-stage investments, entrepreneurship-specific human capital, cutting edge research institutions, lead users of innovations, dense social networks among entrepreneurs, and cultural orientations that are supportive of entrepreneurial activities" (Roundy, 2019, p. 9). Of which, cultural orientations, social norms, and beliefs support the initiative taking aspect of the entrepreneurs that is, "who chooses to be an entrepreneur", which is the foremost step in the entrepreneurial journey (The Global Entrepreneurship and Development Institute, 2018). Thus, there is a need to study the Australians perceptions, attitudes, social values, and beliefs (soft framework conditions) as fewer individuals are embarking on the entrepreneurial journey and one potentially preventing factor highlighted by most research and surveys is fear of failure (Australian Government: Department of Industry, Science, Energy, Resources: Office of the Chief Economist, 2020).

Entrepreneurial Activity and Attitudes in Australia

Social values play an integral role in determining individual's entrepreneurial behaviour. "Behind entrepreneurial action are entrepreneurial intentions; Behind entrepreneurial intentions are known entrepreneurial attitudes; Behind entrepreneurial attitudes are deep cognitive structures; Behind deep cognitive structures are deep beliefs" (Kirkley, 2016a, p. 291).

Consequently, Australian's perceptions of entrepreneurship can greatly influence entrepreneurial activity. Recently G20 Roundtable on Entrepreneurship was held, and the topic of discussion was "*Policies and Actions to Promote Entrepreneurship in the post-pandemic era*". All the member countries shared their respective policy measures. With regards to Australia, it was highlighted that Australia has a very strong corporate entrepreneurship which was further supported by findings of Global Entrepreneurship Monitor (GEM) studies which highlighted that between 10.5 and 11.8% of Australians are involved in early-stage entrepreneurial activity. This includes intrapreneurship (entrepreneurs working in a business for an employer), new business ownership, and early or nascent activity. Australia ranks first out of the 50 participating countries for intrapreneurship (Renando, 2020). Thus, the statistics clearly show that Australia's entrepreneur potential is strong, but it is often held inside established institutions focussed on local challenges primarily because of the high fear of failure.

Australia has been ranked 23rd in Global Innovation Index (GII), 2020, which is one position down since 2019. GII ranks the countries according to their innovation capabilities (WIPO, 2020). The 2016 Performance Review of Australia's Innovation and Science System, conducted by Innovation and Science Australia, found that "The process of innovation can be significantly inhibited if failed attempts cannot be openly discussed, evaluated, reviewed or dismantled in a supportive environment in order to inform the next attempt" (Australian Government: Innovation and Science Australia, 2016).

According to the CGU Ambition Index (2018), more than half (53%) of Australians have aspirations to start their own business but have not converted their aspirations to reality because 44% of Australians say that their biggest deterrent is fear of failure, that has stopped them from pursuing aspirations/goals (CGU Ambition Index, 2018). Global Entrepreneurship Monitor (GEM) report 2019 highlights that 45.7% of Australians see good opportunities to start a business but are afraid to fail (Moyle et al., 2020).

It is the entrepreneurs who perceive and pursue opportunities. Opportunities can only be validated if pursued. Thus, it is a trial-and-error process, and it is the entrepreneurs who drive the trial-and-error dynamic (The Global Entrepreneurship and Development Institute,

2018). According to Peter Drucker "entrepreneurship is about taking risk" (Eroğlu & Piçak, 2011, p. 146). An Entrepreneur is a risk bearer; it is a trait that has been extensively highlighted in entrepreneurial literature and has also shown high validity (Shaper et al., 2014) because "entrepreneurial function entails coping up with less structured, more uncertain set of possibilities and bearing the ultimate responsibility for the decision" (Stewart & Roth, 2001, p. 146). Where there is uncertainty there is bound to be an element of failure/failing. Failure leads to a stigmatizing situation as negative attitude towards failure prevails. Therefore, Australia's fear of failure is high and is rising which prevents them from setting up a business. According to the 2016/2017 GEM report, 42.9% of Australians indicated that they have a fear of failure (Ghazavi, 2018). Whereas a recent GEM report highlighted that 47.4% of Australians have a fear of failure which clearly shows that there has been an increase in the fear levels of Australians, because of which they are unwilling to start a business even when they see good opportunities (Moyle et al., 2020).

United States Studies Centre (USSC), Innovation and Entrepreneurship programme a multi-year research initiative funded by New South Wales (NSW) government focussed on understanding the United States as an innovation leader with a view to developing insight for the benefit of New South Wales and Australia, studied into what causes anxiety in Australians, found that they are more concerned about losing their work (job or business), failure at work, and losing everything and having to start from scratch (Ratcliff et al., 2018).

Stewart and Roth (2001, p. 146) highlighted that more risk-tolerant individuals pursue entrepreneurial careers, whereas more risk-averse individuals choose to work for someone or go for contractual employment (Stewart & Roth, 2001, p. 146). Since entrepreneurship is an important source of wealth creation, job creation, and growth, there is a strong need to change the social beliefs and cultures to reduce the social cost associated with business failure. There is a constant need to acknowledge and celebrate successful entrepreneurs (entrepreneurial role-models) as it inspires others to start business ventures (Ucbasaran et al., 2013). At the same time, failed attempts should be openly discussed and reviewed, as until people do not talk or share their failures with the rest of the people, we will not have the "lessons learnt" which is the one thing that makes failure valuable. Societal attitudes help shape a country's entrepreneurial culture, a culture that rewards entrepreneurs and tolerates failure is a missing ingredient in Australia's social capital. It is only when we overcome stigma revolving around failure, we can have these behind entrepreneurs (intrapreneurs) come forward and start their own ventures. Building a culture that encourages and celebrates entrepreneurship is the key as it is this social capital that sustains the entrepreneurial ecosystem (Ghazavi, 2018).

Schools and Universities and career advisors should bring/invite entrepreneurs to their institutions to share their real-life stories of learning from failures. Smith College, the all-women's school in Western Massachusetts, has a programme called "Failing Well". It is an initiative started by Rachel Simmons to teach its students that "failure is not a bug of learning it's the feature". Students who enrol in her programme receive a Certificate of Failure that declares that they are "hereby authorized to screw up, bomb, or fail" at a test, relationship, project, experiment, or any other initiative. Thus, preparing students to handle failure as those who can tackle failure are less fragile and more audacious than those who expect flawless performance (Taylor, 2017). Programmes like these help instil confidence to face failures from the very beginning when one is at the nurturing stage.

A study by Kauffman Foundation in the US found that university students who took part in experiential entrepreneurship programmes like an internship in a technological start-up together with classroom-based knowledge were three times more inclined to be involved in the creation of a new business venture than others. The classroom knowledge provides them with the knowledge and skill that students can put to practice when they start their own business or when they are working as an employee for a company. Experiential entrepreneurship programmes provide a relatively safe environment to the students where they can experience aspects of actually forming a start-up. This environment will not only provide the students with the context to apply classroom knowledge but also instil confidence and will reduce the fear of failure by allowing them to fail fast in a safe environment (Australian Government: Office of the Chief Scientist, 2015). Australia already is on the path of progress as there has been a recent surge in university-based incubators, accelerators, and entrepreneurism courses which have the potential of debunking the negative attitude towards failure (Ghazavi, 2018).

Conclusion

Entrepreneurship is the backbone of any progressive nation or economy as it leads to the creation of jobs, creation of wealth, new products, and services that are introduced in the market. Given its importance, it thus raises some concerns as fewer entrepreneurs were found to be entering the Australian market. As numerous research have highlighted that this trend is somewhere linked to the rising fear of failure which is crippling entrepreneurial spirit amongst Australians. Therefore, there is a strong need to address the issue and reshape the societal values and attitudes that revolve around failure as it is social and cultural context of an individual that influences creation of business.

References

Australian Government: Department of Industry, Science, Energy and Resources. (2020). *Boosting innovation and science*. Retrieved March 16, 2021, from https://www.industry.gov.au/policies-and-initiatives/boosting-innovation-and-science

Australian Government: Department of Industry, Science, Energy, Resources: Office of the Chief Economist. (2020). *Entrepreneurship*. Retrieved March 16, 2021, from https://publications.industry.gov.au/publications/australia ninnovationsystemmonitor/entrepreneurship/index.html

Australian Government: Innovation and Science Australia. (2016). *Performance review of the Australian innovation, science and research system*. Retrieved March 19, 2021, from https://www.industry.gov.au/sites/default/files/2018-10/performance-review-of-the-australian-innovation-science-and-res earch-system-isa.pdf?acsf_files_redirect

Australian Government: Office of the Chief Scientist. (2015, October). *Boosting high-impact entrepreneurship in Australia*. Office of the Chief Scientist.

CGU Ambition Index. (2018, October 29). *CGU ambition index*. Retrieved March 19, 2021, from https://www.cgu.com.au/ambition/CGU_Ambition_Index.pdf

Eisenmann, T. R. (2013). *Entrepreneurship: A working definition*. Retrieved February 20, 2021, from https://hbr.org/2013/01/what-is-entrepreneur ship

Eroğlu, O., & Piçak, M. (2011). Entrepreneurship, national culture and Turkey. *International Journal of Business and Social Science*, *2*(16), 146–151 (p. 146).

Ghazavi, V. (2018). *How Australia can stop fearing failure and embrace the best of American innovation culture*. Retrieved March 16, 2021, from https://

www.ussc.edu.au/analysis/how-australia-can-stop-fearing-failure-and-embrace-the-best-of-american-innovation-culture#footnote-def-20

Kirkley, W. W. (2016a). Entrepreneurial behaviour: The role of values. *International Journal of Entrepreneurial Behavior & Research*, *22*(3), 290–328 (p. 291).

Kirkley, W. W. (2016b). Entrepreneurial behaviour: the role of values. *International Journal of Entrepreneurial Behavior & Research*, *22*(3), 293 (p. 293).

Lazear, E. P. (2005). Entrepreneurship. *Journal of Labor Economics, 23*(4), 649–680.

Maritz, A. (2015). Senior entrepreneurship in Australia: An exploratory approach. *International Journal of Organizational Innovation, 7*(3), 6–23.

Moyle, D. C.-L., Torres de Oliveira, D., Nguyen, D., & Renando, C. (2020). *Global entrepreneurship monitor Australian population survey.* Retrieved February 20, 2021, from https://research.qut.edu.au/ace/gem-australia-national-trends-aps/

Ratcliff, D. S., McFarland, C., Mondschein, J., & Jackman, S. (2018). *Australians as anxious about healthcare costs as Americans, more anxious about climate change.* Retrieved March 15, 2021, from https://www.ussc.edu.au/analysis/australians-as-anxious-about-healthcare-costs-as-americans-more-anxious-about-climate-change

Renando, C. (2020). *The Australian entrepreneur ecosystem: Presentation at the 2020 G20 roundtable on entrepreneurship.* Retrieved March 4, 2021, from https://www.linkedin.com/pulse/australian-entrepreneur-ecosystem-presentation-2020-g20-chad-renando/

Roundy, P. T. (2019). Regional differences in impact investment: A theory of impact investing ecosystems. *Social Responsibility Journal*, *16*(4), 467–485 (p. 9).

Shaper, M., Volery, T., Weber, P., & Gibson, B. J. (2014). Opportunities and entrepreneurs. In *Entrepreneurship and small business* (pp. 29–50). 4th Asia Pacific Edition. Wiley.

Statista. (2020). *Entrepreneurial activity participation in Australia 2019, by business stage Published by Thomas Hinton, Oct 2, 2020 During the survey period in 2019, it was estimated that 10.5 percent of the population aged 18 to 64 years were engaged in early stage ent.* Retrieved February 20, 2021, from https://www.statista.com/statistics/881473/australia-entrepreneurial-activity-participation-by-business-phase/#statisticContainer

Stevenson, H. H. (2000). *Why entrepreneurship has won!* Retrieved February 20, 2021, from http://www.unm.edu/~asalazar/Kauffman/Entrep_research/e_won.pdf

Stewart, W. H., & Roth, P. L. (2001). Risk propensity differences between entrepreneurs and managers: A meta-analytic review. *Journal of Applied Psychology*, *86*(1), 145–153 (p. 146).

Tang, E. (2019). *Doing business in Australia is easier*. Retrieved March 13, 2021, from https://www.austrade.gov.au/news/economic-analysis/doing-business-in-australia-is-easier

Taylor, B. (2017). *How Coca-Cola, Netflix, and Amazon learn from failure*. Retrieved March 16, 2021, from https://hbr.org/2017/11/how-coca-cola-netflix-and-amazon-learn-from-failure

The Global Entrepreneurship and Development Institute. (2018). *Global entrepreneurship index: Entrepreneurship and business statistics*. Retrieved March 13, 2021, from https://thegedi.org/wp-content/uploads/dlm_uploads/2017/11/GEI-2018-1.pdf

Ucbasaran, D., Shepherd, D. A., Lockett, A., & Lyon, S. (2013). Life after business failure: The process and consequences of business failure for entrepreneurs. *Journal of Management, 39*(1), 163–202.

WIPO. (2020). *Global innovation index 2020*. Retrieved March 19, 2021, from https://www.wipo.int/edocs/pubdocs/en/wipo_pub_gii_2020/au.pdf

World Bank. (2019). *Doing business 2020–sustaining the pace of reforms*. Retrieved March 13, 2021, from https://www.worldbank.org/en/news/feature/2019/10/24/doing-business-2020-sustaining-the-pace-of-reforms

CHAPTER 7

Oceania Crisis Management and Resilience

Vanessa Ratten

Introduction

The world's economy was virtually shut down overnight in March 2020 when the World Health Organisation declared COVID-19 a pandemic. The unprecedented impact of COVID-19 meant a change to working from home and increased usage of digital technology (Roper & Turner, 2020). Some industries of the economy such as the tourism and hospitality sector were severely affected by the altering of economic conditions. Further social changes including mask-wearing, location restrictions and social distancing were introduced. These changes resulted in temporary closures of many businesses that were based on direct human interaction or an alteration in business models to a digital format. In addition, many businesses had to limit or restrict their activities based on policy guidelines.

It is widely recognised that the COVID-19 pandemic has brought significant economic, environmental, financial and social change to the global business environment. This has resulted in the COVID-19

V. Ratten (✉)
La Trobe University, Melbourne, Australia
e-mail: v.ratten@latrobe.edu.au

V. Ratten (ed.), *Oceania Entrepreneurship*,
https://doi.org/10.1007/978-981-16-7341-2_7

pandemic forcing a deeper look at how society reacts to crises (Wagstaff et al., 2020). Whilst the reopening of the global economy began in June 2020, subsequent second and third waves of infection required further modifications to the tourism industry. The approval of vaccines in November and December 2020 is further expected to signal a move back to previous business models. However, the pandemic is likely to have a significant impact on Oceania for some time due to the profound changes that occurred in society. Scholars are now expected to include a mention of COVID-19 in their studies.

Originally in December 2019 and January 2020 the World Health Organisation was informed of a cluster of pneumonia patients in Wuhan City, China, that were associated with a novel coronavirus called 2019.nCoV. By the end of January 2020 this coronavirus had spread to other parts of the world. In February 2020 the WHO officially named the coronavirus as COVID-19 and SARS-COV-2 (severe acute respiratory syndrome coronavirus 2). COVID-19 was subsequently described as an infectious disease that triggered respiratory illness. Due to the highly infectious nature of COVID-19 it was declared a pandemic and recognised as a global crisis. Crises typically are confined to a specific geographic area or time period and are less likely to have an ongoing effect. The continued and uncertain nature of COVID-19 has meant it has been difficult for global business to adapt due to the crisis having global implications. This means that simultaneous action in terms of economic and social considerations are required for the tourism industry. Thus, business research practice and policy on COVID-19 is of increasing relevance for society (Venkatesh, 2020). This chapter attempts to assess how COVID-19 has affected the global economy by focussing on the interlinked needs of stakeholders in Oceania.

As indicated earlier research on COVID-19 is in its nascent stage and still emerging. This is due to the recent nature of the COVID-19 pandemic and uncertainty about its future effect on the global economy. Much of the current research primarily focusses on exploring the impact of COVID-19 on society from a number of different contexts. Very few studies investigate the entrepreneurial outcomes of COVID-19 in terms of developing new products and services. This makes it a timely topic in terms of thinking about future research and practice pathways. Moreover, the current research exploring COVID-19 and entrepreneurship has produced inconsistent findings with positive, negative and neutral results being found. This means there is still much debate about the effects of COVID-19 on the global business industry.

This chapter advances increased interest in the way crises influence entrepreneurial behaviour. By focussing on how the COVID-19 pandemic has played out new directions in the entrepreneurship literature are identified. This means addressing questions such as "How has the COVID-19 pandemic affected Oceania?," "How has existing crisis and resilience research informed our understanding about the COVID-19 pandemic?" and "Can entrepreneurship research help alleviate problems caused by COVID-19?." These questions are answered in the next sections that discuss crisis management and resilience.

Crisis Management

A crisis involves any occurrence that threatens the normal operations of businesses. This includes a disruption that changes the current way business is conducted. The crisis is subjective as it depends on the interpretation of others as to its severity (Bhaduri, 2019). Crises damage the economy by causing an economic downturn. This interrupts the continuity of the economy and influences its reputation. Due to the impact of a crisis, the viability of businesses is threatened. This makes it difficult for businesses to survive and then recover from the negative impacts. Some crises occur quickly and the recovery is fast but others damage entire ecosystems and take time to repair (Comfort, 2007). Ritchie and Jiang (2019) suggest that a crisis can be divided into three main stages: (1) preparedness and planning, (2) response and recovery and (3) result and reflection. The first stage involves being prepared for a crisis in terms of developing a proactive response. This can reduce the potential impact of a crisis. To do this there needs to be crisis management strategies in place. This will enable better coordination amongst stakeholders. Moreover, as part of planning for a crisis there needs to be some form of risk assessment (Branicki, 2020). This will involve the use of forecasting tools to detect potential crises. The second stage involves response and recovery. This means learning about the crisis and then implementing appropriate response actions. This can involve communication about a crisis and then establishing market recovery strategies. This might involve new market segmentation and community collaboration. As part of the recovery process, it can also be useful to establish education initiatives around how to be resilient. The third stage involves resolution and reflection. This means managing knowledge about the crisis in order to anticipate future crises.

Crises are characterised by their extreme nature and unpredictability. This makes planning for their occurrence difficult due to the complexity behind scenario forecasts (Ratten & Dana, 2017). To respond to a crisis properly there needs to be effective communication mechanisms in the community. This enables public administrators to organise a response then to communicate its development to the public. During a crisis there is likely to be different levels of support needed so public officials need to provide surge capacity (Ratten, 2011). In a crisis resources including finance, goods and people need to be mobilised (Pearson & Mitroff, 1983). This means that an effective resource mobilisation strategy is required. Moreover, specific resources needs of entities affected by the crisis should be considered.

Labour market strategies have been implemented to manage the crisis. Workplaces have adopted prevention and protection measures including working from home. When in-person work is needed, social distancing and hand hygiene have been required. Moreover, the use of facemasks has been made compulsory and there has been the introduction of temperature checks at the entrance and exits of workplaces. Many governments have subsidised the wages of workers who have had to quarantine. Therefore, more research is needed on analysing the effectiveness of different COVID-19 strategies. This includes comparing and contrasting before and after situations.

During COVID-19 countries have had to weigh up the social and economic costs of lockdowns. This produces a dilemma as lockdowns can reduce pressure on healthcare systems but produce other effects. Lockdowns have been the primary strategy used by governments to suppress transmission of the disease. Due to only recently vaccines being approached previous non-pharmaceutical methods such as lockdowns were the preferred method. Lockdowns are a short-term strategy and whilst they have occurred at multiple times they do not present a long-term solution. They enable governments to buy time for preparing health services and changing societal conduct. As a result of these lockdowns, the spread of the virus has decreased and enabled a flattening of the curve. The global economy is expected to contract and fall into a long recession as a result of these lockdowns. Countries that are reliant on tourism in Oceania such as Fiji are expected to be more affected by the global lockdown restrictions. Sectors of the economy that can work from home such as information technology and online services are expected to increase due to the COVID-19 pandemic.

It is important to review the past history of the COVID-19 crisis in order to capture where we have been then to think about the future and new possibilities. This enables a better understanding about the relationship between COVID-19 and entrepreneurship. Crises can take a number of different forms including financial (e.g. the 2008 global financial crisis, the 1930'1 Great Depression), natural (hurricane Katrina in 2015), terrorism (September 11, 2001) or military (World War 1 and World War II). During the crisis a different approach to business is needed. This means changing existing business practices to take into account emerging contexts. Crisis research has tended to take a general management approach and has therefore been understudied in the entrepreneurship research. Whilst this is changing due to the COVID-19 pandemic, there is still some way to go before there is a substantial body of research on COVID-19 and entrepreneurship.

A crisis by definition represents an extreme event that will take some time to solve. This differentiates it from an emergency that has a more shorter time period. Crises require an urgent response and create a dilemma as to how to solve them (Ratten, 2010). This means there is some ambiguity as to the best approach to take during a crisis. Looking back after a crisis has occurred means there is the benefit of hindsight (Kang et al., 2021). This enables better decisions to be made as there is more information available about potential consequences. Pearson and Clair (1998, p. 66) define a crisis as "a low-probability, high-impact situation that is perceived by critical stakeholders to threaten the viability of the organisation". This definition acknowledges the rarity of a crisis but also stresses its impact. A crisis if not handled in the right way can cause irreparable damage. This makes it important to consider handling a crisis in an urgent manner. A crisis can be described as a process as it can change over time (Williams et al., 2017). This means the normal functioning of an organisation in a crisis changes based on the environmental context (Jones et al., 2017). The disturbance felt from a crisis can mean a need to rethink an organisation's strategic direction.

Resilience

In order to cope with crises, businesses need to be resilient. Resilience is defined as "the capacity to cope with unanticipated dangers after they have become manifest, learning to bounce back" (Wildavsky, 1988, p. 77). Increasingly businesses are trying to be more resilient in order to adapt to new environmental contexts. This means resilience is often viewed as a psychological orientation towards change. This is evident in Luthans (2002, p. 702) suggesting that resilience is the "positive psychological capacity to rebound, to 'bounce back' from adversity, uncertainty, conflict, failure, or even positive change, progress and increased responsibility". Therefore, having the capacity to foresee change and view it in a positive way is important in today's global business environment. Coutu (2002, p. 52) describes resilience as "the skill and the capacity to be robust under conditions of enormous stress and change". This means that resilience is a dynamic trait that can be learnt over time. Thus, as circumstances change, an individual can develop their resilience capability. Hamel and Valikangas (2004, p. 355) describe resilience as "the ability to dynamically reinvent business models and strategies as circumstances change, to continuously anticipate and adjust to changes that threaten their core earning power- and to change before the need becomes desperately obvious". This definition highlights that individuals need to continually readjust before the change is required. Thereby sensing alterations in the environment and then making steps to adjust. To overcome exposure to adversity it helps to be adaptive. This skill enables a positive response to emerge from a potential threat. As individuals do not exist in isolation, resilience can be considered a social factor. This means individual attitudes to change are influenced by collective outcomes. Thereby individuals and community goals are intertwined. Through collective interaction, individuals utilise social resources to respond to change.

Resilience is a behavioural characteristic that helps prevent crises. Williams et al. (2017, p. 742) describes resilience as "the process by which an actor (ie individual, organization, or community) builds and uses its capability endowments to interact with the environment in a way that positively adjusts and maintains functioning prior to, during and following adversity". This involves having a capacity to prevent adversity before it becomes necessary to change. Resilience is a way for entities to be proactive about potential transformational activity. In this way, the disruption does not threaten survival but rather is a hurdle that needs to be overcome.

Resilience involves anticipating then reacting to market changes. This is important due to the dynamic nature of the global business environment that requires entities to constantly adapt. Some organisations are able to thrive despite adversity but others perish. This means building skills that help an organisation deal with uncertainty is important. Inevitably all organisations will deal with some form of adversity. This adversity strains their business functions and can lead to a deacceleration of demand. To cope with adversity organisations need to be resilient. This enables the maintenance of existing conditions when an organisation faces challenging conditions.

Resilience is a fuzzy concept as definitive skill sets are still unknown (Vakilzadeh & Haase, 2021). All organisations regardless of their industry context face some degree of turbulence. This means they need to develop an organisational culture based on being able to quickly adapt and change. During times of uncertainty, being resilient is a positive organisational trait. The ability of organisations to deal with change depends both on internal and external factors. Internal factors relate to the ability of leaders to enact provisions to deal with the change. External factors relate more to environmental changes in the industry or country context. Resilience occurs when "an organisation, or indeed a team or individual, demonstrates a positive outcome following an unexpected or disruptive event" (Fasey et al., 2021, p. 1). This means in times of crisis being resilient can enable businesses to survive.

Resilience is a way to positively adapt when experiencing times of adversity. To develop team resilience it helps to have team members who inspire and motivate others to take responsibility. Team resilience is defined as "a dynamic psychosocial process which protects a group of individuals form the potential negative effect of the stressors they collectively encounter" (Morgan et al., 2013, p. 552). This ensures a selfless culture that is based on togetherness as a team. Another type of resilience involves organisations that are able to adapt to change. Organisational resilience is defined as "the maintenance of positive adjustment under challenging conditions such that the organisation emerges from those conditions strengthened and more resourceful" (Vogus & Sutcliffe, 2007, p. 3418). This definition emphasises the need for an organisation to continually adapt by rethinking its current strategy. This involves adopting new innovations in a way that progresses the overall objective of an organisation.

Another definition by Burnard and Bhamra (2011, p. 5587) also stresses the need for adaptability in organisations by suggesting that organisational resilience involves "the inherent and adaptive qualities and capabilities that enable an organisation's adaptive capacity during turbulent periods". This means there is an expectation of periods of uncertainty that are difficult to predict. The uncertainty is normally viewed as an extreme event that potentially can have disastrous effects. Therefore, it becomes important to carefully handle a crisis by taking a resilient attitude. This ensures the disruption whilst causing negative effects can also have a positive outcome.

Anticipation of a crisis means that organisation's need to accept that there will be periods of disruption. This means preparing for them as best they can be based on the resources available. Once they accept this inevitability they can then design a strategic plan. This involves thinking about solutions and steps needed in order to rectify the situation. Once the crisis has occurred then they can implement solutions based on priority and need. After the crisis has occurred then they can also reflect and learn about how to do things better in the future. This means learning from experience that will enable an organisation to implement solutions. Organisations need to preserve relationships in a crisis by having good business models. This enables them to gain help from stakeholders in order to return more quickly to pre-crisis conditions. Organisations cannot prevent crises from occurring, but they can minimise the damage. This means having contingency plans in place that try to predict likely crises scenarios. This foresight will enable them to prepare for adversity. Organisations need to have an open organisational culture in order to facilitate innovative thinking. This will enable novel aspects of a crisis to be solved in a meaningful way. This might involve improvisation that involves some degree of flexibility in terms of how an organisation responds to a crisis. Setbacks from adverse circumstances are a normal occurrence. The experience gained from these events helps individuals to learn and then react better in the future. There is a multitude of stressors occurring in the business environment at any point in time. These events can enable new business opportunities to open up in the marketplace.

Resilience refers to adaption in the context of adversity. The adaptation involves a setback that can severely endanger the functioning of an organisation. The severity of these setbacks is based on perception as some setbacks are considered dangerous whilst to others they represent a mild disturbance. Organisations need to deliberately implement strategies to deal with setbacks. These preparatory measures help to anticipate change whilst maintaining the momentum of an organisation. Resilience is a process and requires an organisation to reorientate itself for change. After suffering a setback, resilient organisations should be able to emerge stronger. This is due to the organisation learning new capabilities and skills.

In order to build resilience, individuals need to read cues and build relationships. This enables them to manage crises by focussing on changes in the environment. Being resilient means that an individual can withstand stressors and overcome obstacles. This ability enables individuals in times of crisis to employ necessary resources. By being aware of potential crises, an individuals can make sense of adverse situations and implement solutions. All businesses face challenges but few of these challenges are catastrophic. This means when there is a serious crisis there need to be decisions made about the causes of action to take. Resilience is needed to sustain morale and performance over a long time period. This enables individuals to be robust and overcome stressful situations. This is important in order to manage negative emotions that often come with crises. Adaptive resilience is a psychological trait that enables individuals to manage stretching or extreme events. This means individuals are able to implement effective responses to adversity. As a crisis can be a traumatic event, it helps to develop resilience capability in order to respond to adversity in a positive way.

It is important that individuals are able to deal with competing priorities and time issues. This means managing interpersonal conflicts and unclear processes. This form of risk and stress management is useful in today's business environment that has changing circumstances. If individuals do not respond in the right way, then it can trigger further imbalances and push the individual off track at any time. Individuals can take a proactive approach to be resilient by focussing on non-crisis environments. This enables them to develop skills useful in crises environments that enables continual improvement. Individuals need to understand the mechanisms that facilitate resilience. This enables them to be in a better position when a crisis occurs. Whilst there are everyday risky situations that require risk management strategies, resilience is about being able to deal with crisis situations that require individuals to take action on the go.

Theoretical Implications

The importance of taking a COVID-19 perspective in existing theory is new and not yet fully established in the literature. Mainstream management literature tends to neglect the impact of the crises on organisations and individuals by adopting a general approach. This means existing theories of management treat all contexts as the same and do not acknowledge the effect of the crises. Therefore, there is a clear need for theories that conceptualise and acknowledge the COVID-19 crisis that can help entrepreneurs in Oceania. This will offer more opportunities for the advancement of existing theories that utilise a COVID-19 approach. To generate new theories, theoretical work based on the COVID-19 crisis is required. The management discipline provides rich source of data for new theories to emerge. The typical management theory has been in existence for some time so new developments to these theories are required. Context is a critical aspect of theory development, so the COVID-19 context needs to be incorporated into Oceania entrepreneurship research. This will in turn affect theoretical frameworks that are not premised on crisis situations. Therefore, the COVID-19 context offers several avenues for the development of new theories. Many benefits would result from taking a COVID-19 approach, including the use of relatively recent concepts such as resilience.

Within the entrepreneurship, strategy and management field, the topic of COVID-19 is witnessing an increasing amount of attention, as evidenced, by topic-oriented special journal issues, books and conferences (Gomez et al., 2020). This growing interest can be interpreted in both positive and negative ways. On the positive side, the COVID-19 crisis has led to many changes particularly around digital technology usage in Oceania. For example, more people and businesses have higher levels of digital literacy making possible online transactions (Ferreira et al., 2017b). This helps facilitate the use of digital entrepreneurship in ways not seen before. New business models have emerged that cater for the digital market within or in addition to existing business models (Ferreira et al., 2017a). On the other hand, COVID-19 has led to negative changes in terms of reduced working hours for many people and a need to work from home. Whilst there can be time savings from telecommuting there are also increased pressures in maintaining a work/life balance. Whilst the COVID-19 crisis is recent and ongoing, research on this topic has not received much explicit research attention. The reason for this can be attributed to a lack of available data on the topic in terms of entrepreneurial performance.

One main argument for the need of COVID-19 entrepreneurship studies is based on the potential of new ventures to provide additional sources of revenue. This can counteract the damage COVID-19 has done on the economy. At the moment, there is little overlap between the fields of COVID-19 health research and Oceania entrepreneurship, but there is an increasing body of literature. Recent publications in the COVID-19 field continue to proclaim a lack of entrepreneurship scholarship.

Managerial Implications

In the contemporary global marketplace, managers in Oceania have become aware of how to deal with the COVID-19 crisis. The emphasis has now shifted to be COVID-19 safe and this has created novel management practices. Creating value from COVID-19 conditions can develop favourable consumer perspectives of management performance. This is imperative because managers in Oceania now live under different conditions. There are several steps that businesses need to consider in order to deal with the COVID-19 crisis. Firstly, businesses need to protect themselves, their employees and customers from harm. Consumers who require COVID-19 related products and services constitute a monolithic opportunity for managers. This means they are willing to pay a premium for COVID-19 safe services thereby amplifying the need for covid products.

Resilience is a crisis management tool utilised by the business world. It enables businesses to have a strategy about how they respond to risk. Thereby enabling them to adapt to new market conditions by mitigating potential risks. Resilience is linked to the idea that businesses need to have a flexible and dynamic attitude to exist in the global marketplace. Resilience requires businesses to recognise risks and then to develop timely intervention mechanisms. This involves coordinating different crisis management techniques in a scaleable way. To do this, businesses should have good relationships amongst all stakeholders that ensure a cohesive approach to risk. This means businesses can be proactive instead of reactive when they face adversity. This attitude means the business structure will have a more dynamic approach to how it evaluates risk. The global business environment bounced back after previous epidemics including Ebola, Middle East Respiratory Syndrome (MERS) and Severe Acute Respiratory Syndrome (SARS). However, these epidemics were concentrated in specific geographic locations unlike COVID-19 that has had global implications. This means global business needs to aid recovery by providing incentives for businesses to get back to normal. This means increasing customer and employee engagement that can help in building confidence. Governments in Oceania play a significant role in the economy by providing stimulus packages and interventions.

The COVID-19 pandemic has meant years of international business linkages and globalisation are in jeopardy. This has meant countries in Oceania have had to rethink their trade relationships due to rising national interest sentiment. Disruptions are a natural part of business but when significant disruptions occur, they have the power to substantially change business practices. The way businesses deal with disruptions depends on attitudes, capabilities and support structures. Some disruptions are foreseeable due to natural catastrophes occurring on a frequent basis. Other forms of disruptions are less frequent and come as complete surprises. This means businesses need to engage in scenario planning in order to help understand the probability of certain events occurring in the market. This will help make it easier to manage disruptions if they occur. The COVID-19 pandemic is at the moment an ongoing crisis with no definite end date. Similar to previous health crises even when there is a vaccine it takes time for the global population to be inoculated. The interruption caused by COVID-19 is unresolved and will require government and business involvement in order to be solved. This means there are likely to be lasting consequences for the global economy arising from the COVID-19 pandemic. Increased levels of internationalisation have meant easier cross-border travel contributed to the spread of COVID-19. This meant that the interdependencies of countries multiplied the effect of the virus.

Conclusion

This chapter has discussed the role of crises management and resilience. These topics are important in the current global business environment for businesses in Oceania that want to stay competitive. The impact of crisis on entrepreneurial behaviour was highlighted in this chapter thereby offering a way of understanding the role change plays in a business context. Theoretical and managerial implications were also stated that stress the need for futuristic thinking.

References

Bhaduri, R. M. (2019). Leveraging culture and leadership in crisis management. *European Journal of Training and Development, 43*(5/6), 554–569.

Branicki, L. (2020). COVID-19, ethics of care and feminist crisis management. *Gender, Work and Organization, 27*, 872–883.

Burnard, K., & Bhamra, R. (2011). Organisational resilience: Development of a conceptual framework for organisational responses. *International Journal of Production Research, 49*(18), 5581–5599.

Comfort, L. K. (2007). Crisis management in hindsight: Cognition, communication, coordination, and control. *Public Administration Review, 67*, 189–197.

Coutu, D. L. (2002). How resilience works. *Harvard Business Review, 80*(5), 46–56.

Fasey, K. J., Sarkar, M., Wagstaff, C. R., & Johnston, J. (2021). Defining and characterizing organizational resilience in elite sport. *Psychology of Sport and Exercise, 52*, 101834.

Ferreira, J. J., Fernandes, C. I., & Ratten, V. (2017a). Entrepreneurship, innovation and competitiveness: What is the connection? *International Journal of Business and Globalisation, 18*(1), 73–95.

Ferreira, J. J., Ratten, V., & Dana, L. P. (2017b). Knowledge spillover-based strategic entrepreneurship. *International Entrepreneurship and Management Journal, 13*(1), 161–167.

Gomez, S., Mendoza, O., Ramirez, J., & Olivas-Lujan, M. (2020). Stress and myths related to the COVID-19 pandemic's effects on remote work. *Management Research: Journal of the Iberoamerican Academy of Management, 18*(4), 401–420.

Hamel, G., & Valikangas, L. (2004). The quest for resilience. *icade. Revista De La Facultad De Derecho, 62*, 355–358.

Jones, P., Jones, A., Williams-Burnett, N., & Ratten, V. (2017). Let's get physical: Stories of entrepreneurial activity from sports coaches/instructors. *The International Journal of Entrepreneurship and Innovation, 18*(4), 219–230.

Kang, J., Diao, Z., & Zanini, M. (2021). Business-to-business marketing responses to COVID-19 crisis: A business process perspective. *Marketing Intelligence & Planning, 39*(3), 454–468.

Luthans, F. (2002). The need for and meaning of positive organizational behavior. *Journal of Organizational Behavior: The International Journal of Industrial, Occupational and Organizational Psychology and Behavior, 23*(6), 695–706.

Morgan, P. B., Fletcher, D., & Sarkar, M. (2013). Defining and characterizing team resilience in elite sport. *Psychology of Sport and Exercise, 14*(4), 549–559.

Pearson, C. M., & Clair, J. A. (1998). Reframing crisis management. *Academy of Management Review, 23*(1), 59–76.

Pearson, C. M., & Mitroff, I. I. (1993). From crisis prone to crisis prepared: A framework for crisis management. *Academy of Management Perspectives, 7*(1), 48–59.
Ratten, V. (2010). The future of sports management: A social responsibility, philanthropy and entrepreneurship perspective. *Journal of Management & Organization, 16*(4), 488–494.
Ratten, V. (2011). Social entrepreneurship and innovation in sports. *International Journal of Social Entrepreneurship and Innovation, 1*(1), 42–54.
Ratten, V., & Dana, L. P. (2017). Sustainable entrepreneurship, family farms and the dairy industry. *International Journal of Social Ecology and Sustainable Development (IJSESD), 8*(3), 114–129.
Ritchie, B. W., & Jiang, Y. (2019). A review of research on tourism risk, crisis and disaster management: Launching the annals of tourism research curated collection on tourism risk, crisis and disaster management. *Annals of Tourism Research, 79*, 102812.
Roper, S., & Turner, J. (2020). R&D and innovation after COVID-19: What can we expect? A review of prior research, and data trends after the great financial crisis. *International Small Business Journal, 38*(6), 504–514.
Vakilzadeh, K., & Haase, A. (2021). The building blocks of organizational resilience: A review of the empirical literature. *Continuity & Resilience Review, 3*(1), 1–21.
Venkatesh, V. (2020). Impacts of COVID-19: A research agenda to support people in their fight. *International Journal of Information Management, 55*, 102197.
Vogus, T. J., & Sutcliffe, K. M. (2007, October). Organizational resilience: Towards a theory and research agenda. In *2007 IEEE International Conference on Systems, Man and Cybernetics* (pp. 3418–3422). IEEE.
Wagstaff, M., Salvaj, E., & Villanueva, S. (2020). Champions in the time of COVID-10: Tracing paths to recovery in IberoAmerica. *Management Research: Journal of the Iberoamerican Academy of Management, 18*(4), 379–399.
Wildavsky, A. (1988). *Searching for safety*. Transaction Books.
Williams, T. A., Gruber, D. A., Sutcliffe, K. M., Shepherd, D. A., & Zhao, E. Y. (2017). Organizational response to adversity: Fusing crisis management and resilience research streams. *Academy of Management Annals, 11*(2), 733–769.

CHAPTER 8

Tourism Innovation in Oceania

Vanessa Ratten

Introduction

Tourism as a process can be viewed as "a sub-set of a vast and heterogeneous complex global mobilities, which also includes migration, return migration, transnationalism, diasporas and other obligatory as well as voluntary forms of travelling" (Cohen & Cohen, 2012, p. 2181). This makes tourism a phenomenon of everyday life as it is based on social conditions and context. Edensor (2001, p. 71) refers to tourism as "a collection of commonly understood and embodied practices and meanings, which are reproduced by tourists through their performances—in alliance with tourist managers and workers". Therefore, tourism should be considered in a broad manner as it involves the interaction of humans and non-humans in a systemic way.

The tourism industry involves a constellation of entities that are involved in the production of a task. The tourism industry differs from other industries as it is service-intensive and involves many public/private partnerships. This means the tourism industry is constantly changing

V. Ratten (✉)
La Trobe University, Melbourne, Australia
e-mail: v.ratten@latrobe.edu.au

V. Ratten (ed.), *Oceania Entrepreneurship*,
https://doi.org/10.1007/978-981-16-7341-2_8

based on market demands and consumer attitudes. Zach and Racherla (2011, p. 97) state that "tourism is a complex phenomenon that cannot be explained by conventional economic or business logic". Therefore, in order to provide consumer services tourism organizations need to both collaborate but also compete with each other. This process is called coopetition and is common in the tourism industry.

Tourism is a product of a multiple number of entities working together to provide a service. This means when an individual travels to a destination the quality of the destination will be based on the coordination of different tourism bodies. Thus, the tourism product can be considered as a value chain in which entities provide services in order to produce an experience. Tourism requires the input of numerous stakeholders in order to function properly. Each stakeholder has its own resources and needs so it can be a complex task to get all stakeholders working together. Tourism stakeholders are needed for destination management reasons. A destination can be considered as "a series of interrelated activities and attractions that have to work in unison to create a satisfying and wholesome experience" (Zach & Racheria, 2011, p. 99). This means a destination considers multiple entities that work in tandem to produce a tourism experience. This experience needs to be delivered in person and at a specific point in time. Therefore, it is a service and cannot be consumed later.

The field of tourism in general has matured as a topic of interest. This is due to the continual growth of studies on tourism from a variety of perspectives. Nonetheless, there is still a gap in the literature about country-level phenomena that challenge current conceptualizations. This means tourism is enacted through various cultural practices in a region. The tourism industry needs to take a proactive stance in planning for change (Asero et al., 2016). This means anticipating change but also acting as an instigator of change. Rising income levels have fostered the demand for tourism (Halme, 2001). This has resulted in tourism being closely linked to context as people travel to regions due to their environmental characteristics. Normally tourist spots tend to be near attractive features of the environment. Moreover, unprecedented demographic changes including the aging population and urbanization levels have led to an increase in tourism (Gibson et al., 2005). This is due to greater emphasis being placed on leisure activity and well-being. This has led to a rise in tourism retreats that cater to these needs.

The global tourism industry is extensive and covers multiple different country contexts (Dredge, 2006). Thus, in order to obtain a better understanding about specific contexts it helps to take a geographic perspective. This enables more detailed information to emerge about how culture influences tourism policy. The aim of this chapter is to focus on Oceania. The diaspora of Oceania people also influences the nature of global tourism. Studying this region is useful as it enables best practices to emerge. Moreover, due to the geographical position of this region it is useful to compare and contrast tourism policy. This is not normally done as there has been a tendency to consider tourism as a collective without considering any form of regional difference. Oceania is a unique region due to its distinct culture and heritage that is endemic in the way tourism is practised and consumed.

There has been an increased emphasis on tourism innovation by global scholars but not enough emphasis on the regional context (Chung et al., 2020). This means there is a stereotype that tourism innovation is the same everywhere when in reality it is not. The context does matter as culture influences the orientation tourism providers have towards innovation. Studies often do not disclose the cultural considerations around tourism innovation. This means there is a lack of understanding about the cause and nature of the tourism innovation. Researchers should discuss in their research whether tourism innovation in Oceania differs from other country contexts. This would help in building a theory of tourism innovation that is specific to Oceania and the diaspora community. By focussing on the country context, it can also enable more detailed case studies to emerge in the literature. This would enable an understanding of the type of tourism innovation in terms of purposeful or opportunistic. Providing more details about how tourism innovation emerges a better theory can be developed. Not all innovation is the same so careful consideration about the climatic and political effects are needed.

Tourism Innovation

The tourism industry is amongst the most innovative industries in the world as it has to continually evolve to suit new consumer preferences. This means innovation is at the centre of any successful change that occurs in the tourism industry. The innovations do not have to be substantial as they can be small or incremental and build on previously existing innovations. However, they do have to be new or be viewed in a creative way.

The concept of tourism innovation has gained considerable legitimacy both in practice and in research (Hjalager, 2009). In practice, innovative tourism providers have paved the way for economic growth and regional development. As an applied field, tourism studies seek to develop advice for practitioners. This means most research on tourism has a concurrent practical relevance. Thereby any study on tourism will have a prominent position amongst real-world practitioners.

In a research setting, academia has partnered with regional policy-makers to provide creative services. However, despite its usefulness there still is a widespread misunderstanding about its core rationale. This is due to the concept being broadly defined in terms of positive change occurring in a tourism setting and lacking a coherent definition. In this chapter, I define tourism innovation also from a positive perspective but emphasise the social change that also occurs. Thereby, taking a more community and societal perspective of tourism innovation.

Tourism innovation is critical in the current knowledge economy, which requires tourism providers to create new business structures and concepts in order to remain competitive (Dolnicar & Ring, 2014). The latest approaches to tourism tend to emphasise information technology, COVID-19 and sustainability practices. In an increasingly global world, the survival of tourism providers depends on their competitive intelligence, which is the result of market knowledge (Cassel & Pashkevich, 2014). Strategic market knowledge refers to the futuristic processes tourism providers use to make key decisions. This includes the use of knowledge to create and share new market developments.

Tourism is amongst the fastest growing industries in the world but it can produce positive as well as negative effects. The positive effects include an increase in gross domestic production and economic output. This enables spillovers from tourism to affect other areas of the economy including education and manufacturing. Tourism can also result in urban regeneration that attracts new businesses and individuals to an area. This provides additional employment opportunities and has a flow-on effect to enhance the livelihood of members of society. The negative effects can include environmental damage and increased traffic flows to an area. This might result in increased costs for local citizens. Moreover, tourism is often seasonal so there may be risks associated with relying on one industry. Some of the negative effects of tourism can be mitigated through education programmes that result in an increased awareness of a place. This can promote ecologically and sustainable forms of tourism.

The importance of knowledge exchange amongst tourism providers has long been widely recognised as a significant phenomenon (McKercher & Du Cros, 2003). The innovation level of the tourism industry relies on this knowledge for its ongoing success (Hjalager, 2010). Thus, cooperation between tourism providers can stimulate the production of new knowledge and technology. Tourism companies are constantly under pressure to change, which makes innovation important to their competitiveness. The effectiveness of innovation depends on the interactions between tourism companies, consumers and institutions (Kahn, 2018). When this interaction becomes progressively more active, tourism innovation has a strong effect on competitiveness. Therefore, tourism innovation and its contribution to the global economy remains high on current government agendas.

In recent years, the increased demand for tourism has led to the reconfiguration of existing tourism businesses in order to foster innovation. This trend, in turn, has been complemented by technology entrepreneurship and changing socio-demographic demands. Thus, tourism innovation creates environments in which tourism providers can exploit opportunities in order to promote innovative phenomena. Through their position in the community tourism providers are no longer considered in isolation but as members of an ecosystem. This means increasingly there are other stakeholders involved in the tourism industry.

The Tourism Industry

Tourism is a field of study that has its roots in anthropology and sociology but more recently has taken a business management perspective. This is due to the tourism industry being globally significant and affecting many other areas of society (Caalders, 1997). Tourism represents an individual's need for adventure and to discover new knowledge. Depending on the preference of the tourist, this knowledge can take a variety of different forms including cultural, educational and historical. Tourism is a temporary interaction between a guest and host that involves a number of stakeholders. This means tourism is not of a permanent nature and is dynamic based on social conditions. There are a variety of entities involved in providing tourism services and infrastructure, which includes public authorities including regional governments and private organizations. Thus, tourism is a complex phenomenon as it requires the input of many stakeholders (Paget et al., 2010). Tourism providers are making better use of stakeholders by engaging in network relationships.

There are a variety of ways tourism networks can be categorised including linkages, exchanges and membership of a group. Tourism networks provide a number of benefits including knowledge transfer and accelerating the pace of business development. Morrison et al. (2004, p. 198) define a tourism network as "a set of formal, co-operative relationships between organisations and individuals to achieve a particular purpose within the tourism sector that may result in qualitative and/or quantitative benefits of a learning and exchange, business activity and/or community nature relative to building profitable tourism destinations". This means the reason for the network is based on the idea of collaboration, cooperation and reciprocity (Chesbrough, 2003). The collaboration often takes the form of public/private partnerships that enable government entities to join forces with companies on a project. This enables the harnessing of joint capabilities that foster better performance outcomes (Feranita et al., 2017). Central to the idea of a network is that there is some degree of cooperation. It is assumed that this cooperation produces positive outcomes but this might not always be true as some results may be negative. Therefore, the idea of reciprocity is also an element of any kind of network relationship (Gërguri-Rashiti et al., 2017). This enables entities in a network to expect help in the future when they have previously helped a network member. This produces a sense of solidarity in the network by emphasising mutual gain.

Individuals are motivated to travel for a variety of reasons some personal whilst others for business reasons. As more people have greater levels of disposable income, people are searching for new ways to be entertained. Tourism providers have stepped into this market by providing entertainment services. Tourism as a sector is a set of interlinked entities that deliver an experience. Due to continual changes in expectations regarding tourism these entities need to adapt. Tourism innovation is a way to describe how entities shape change. It can be hard for tourism providers to adapt due to financial and time restrictions. This makes it important to consider how tourism operators are restricted by their environmental conditions. Tourism is valuable for communities due to the economic gain it provides. However, not all tourism is positive as it can lead to adverse effects. This means that in order to provide a positive impact on society, innovation is an essential part of the tourism industry. Tourism providers need to be innovative in order to be seen as an attractive service (Heiskala, 2007). To do this tourism providers utilise innovation processes that are driven by knowledge acquired about changing conditions. Innovation is a cumulative set of changes that are implemented in a business setting. These iterative changes enable alterations to occur that result in new market conditions.

Due to the increased amount of leisure time people have, the level of international tourism has increased (Ratten, 2011). This has made the study and practice of tourism a popular subject. Initially tourism was only conducted by wealthy individuals who had the resources and time to do so. This has changed with the growing number of middle class who have time to travel. Moreover, changing work practices such as mandatory holiday leave has altered societal practices towards tourism. Tourism can come in a variety of forms including cultural, work and sport (Kokkranikal & Morrison, 2011). This means when studying tourism one has to consider the context. In addition, the nature of tourism is changing with an increased usage of technological innovations.

Tourism as a topic is not just about holidays as it covers transportation and other associated activities (Ratten, 2016). Moreover, regions are focussing on tourism due to the economic gain it brings. This means tourism marketing campaigns have increased as regions increase their competitiveness. Tourism essentially means visiting an area outside of one's home. However, the difference between visiting and tourism is due to the length of time a tourist stays in a region being longer than a visitor. A tourist spends a greater amount of time in the area. People travel for various reasons that influence the time and duration of their stay. Thus, there are so many different types of tourism that it is difficult to define all of them.

Country-Specific Tourism Theory

It is becoming quite clear that most of today's tourism theories are generalised and not country-specific. This results in theories inadequately moving scholarship and practice where it needs to be for tourism entities to cope in the global marketplace. Whilst a generalised tourism theory makes it easy to use, it lacks contextual relevance. This means tourism researchers need to incorporate cultural elements within theory in order to make it more appropriate. Fundamental long-term efforts are required to do this in order to move our understanding of tourism innovation to a new level. Tourism in Oceania is a major contributor to economic growth. The tourism industry in Oceania is amongst the most popular in the world and is amongst the most visited countries. Due to the high quality of life and cultural history, tourists are attracted to Oceania. Beach tourism generates a large percentage of overall income for the Oceanian economy. Moreover, the large coastline and warm climate attract tourists from around the world.

The tourism field needs to move forward to a new stage of academic and practical endeavour by incorporating country insights. Culture and especially human awareness of its effects impinges on all forms of tourism innovation (Ramadani et al., 2015). There has been great progress made in understanding tourism innovation as part of a business process, which has enabled scholars to better understand the full complexity of the issues tourism entities face. Despite this theoretical advancement there is still a long way to go. Tourism innovation continues to be an ever-growing topic. In an era dominated by innovation and characterised by digital change, it is natural that the focus of tourism management has shifted to an innovation perspective (Tajeddini et al., 2017b).

The success and impact of tourism innovation research reflect its scientific rigour and practical relevance. Consequently, tourism scholars pay close attention to theory and practice implications when designing and conducting research. The concurrent need to be practical but also scientific sets tourism research apart from other fields of research (Tajeddini & Ratten, 2020). This alignment keeps tourism research at the front of research studies due to its innovation. Despite these advantages there is a tendency for generalization in theory development without considering the context. This means that whilst the field as a whole has grown, there is diminished geographical relevance. This misalignment plagues the development of the field that is struggling to provide a more inclusive approach. In order to secure more contextual relevance, it helps to consider the cultural and social conditions in a region.

An integrated approach to tourism research is required in order to develop new ideas. This is important as the integration of different disciplines can provide a more holistic approach. This enables the discovery of alternative ways of thinking and connects new to existing research. Interdisciplinary research involves becoming aware of different approaches that would not be evident if only focussing on one discipline. The tourism field whilst rooted in economic geography and regional development relates closely to other disciplines such as innovation and entrepreneurship. Moreover, interdisciplinary approaches can contribute to societal development by exploring problems in a new way. This enables the inherent complexity between nature and society to be emphasised. Thereby producing revolutionary insights that connect disparate elements of society. By breaking down boundaries between fields then-new knowledge can be derived. This enables true transformation to occur that is a by-product of theoretical integration. To address and explore tourism phenomena an integrated approach is required.

Current paradigms regarding tourism research focus mostly on assumptions associated with economic models of behaviour that stereotype all country contexts as being the same. Not all countries have the same tourism practices due to the influence of institutional, political and social structures. Whilst there is research combining a social science perspective it is lacking in quantity in order to make a substantial contribution. This is changing as tourism research takes on a more anthropological and sociological underpinning that recognises the role culture plays in tourism. Therefore, there has been more recent efforts to broaden this horizon by incorporating innovation. More critically, tourism in any form has some degree of innovation either in a direct or indirect format. This enables the core idea of tourism as an economic activity to be considered also as a social or environmental need. This implies that tourism needs to consider the natural environment but also inequality and other problems.

Heritage Tourism

Heritage tourism is integral to understanding any form of tourism in Oceania and is based on the use of inherited assets that have a cultural value. These assets are sociocultural in nature as they connect the present to previous cultures. Heritage tourism includes a wide variety of themes including activities that represent the past (Moulin & Boniface, 2001). This means visiting landscapes and museums that have a historic nature. Heritage tourism provides a way of reconstructing the past. This enables people to explore prior ways of living or events. Heritage is a form of cultural product and is essential to maintaining links to the past. The preservation of culture in society is considered as heritage. Understanding heritage is a reason why many people travel. With travel becoming relatively cheaper and people having more leisure time, travelling to heritage regions has increased.

There can be sometimes tensions in preserving heritage sites whilst bringing a modern approach. The concept of heritage means transferring something from one generation to the next. This means telling stories about the past in order to preserve the cultural traditions of society (Tajeddini et al., 2017a). Tourism as a concept is fluid as it changes based on context (Zach & Racherla, 2011). This means tourism is more of a modern-day activity although it existed in the past. Tradition is part of a region's heritage and the reason why people may visit a region. Heritage tourism enables a way to experience the past but in the present day. This means the portrayal of the past can be interpreted in different ways. There are endless possibilities of interpreting the past, so it is important that heritage tourism providers try to be authentic. Thus, it is useful to research past conditions and then trying to recreate these conditions in the present. By using imagination, the past can be recreated in different ways with the help of modern-day technology.

Built heritage refers to the preservation of physical buildings. This includes monuments, churches and other houses that were significant in the past. Architecture is timebound so it is important to preserve buildings that are based on specific architectural styles. This will enable art forms to be preserved that show distinctive ways of life. Natural heritage refers to outdoor areas that have not been made by humans. This includes parks, gardens and mountains. The natural area includes fauna and flora that showcase animal life. Often these animals have cultural components in terms of linking into a region's folklore. Cultural heritage includes the customs and languages endemic to an area. Built heritage can be analysed in terms of material elements that are of a fixed, semi-fixed or non-fixed nature. Fixed elements cannot be moved and are built around a specific area.

Whilst most forms of heritage are cultural or nature-based, there are also industrial forms. Industrial heritage tourism is defined as "the development of touristic activities and industries on man-made sites, buildings and landscapes that originate with industrial processes of earlier periods" (Edwards & Llurdés, 1996, p. 342). More people are interested in visiting industrial landscapes that show how previous industrial activity took place. This means previously unused areas that were once derelict are being transformed into tourist attractions. Former rustbelts are being changed into tourism meccas thereby bringing financial revenue to regions (Czakon & Czernek, 2016). This helps regions restructure and to profit from tourist activity.

Tourism has flourished due to individuals having increased levels of disposable income (Björk & Virtanen, 2005). Moreover, enhanced international relations and quicker transportation methods have made it easier to travel. Tourism affects every community in the world either in a direct or indirect way. Directly it brings revenues into areas that are an important income stream. Many regions rely on tourism for financial gain and to give employment to local citizens (Caalders, 1997). It also brings additional revenue through associated activities such as taxes and tariffs. Indirectly it influences the strategic direction of an area and the services it decides to focus on. Tourism is a product of supply and demand. It is complex to describe and define as it constantly changes. The most popular forms of tourism include nature, shopping, beach and sport. Heritage tourism is amongst the oldest forms of travel. People have travelled for a long time to destinations that are of cultural importance. Heritage tourism involves seeing the past through the cultural landscape. This can occur by visiting places where interesting cultures exist. Heritage conservation is a priority area for society due to the interest in historical places. This means the preservation of places of a nostalgic importance is valued in society. Some cultural places are hard to conserve due to the impact of humans and the natural environment.

Innovation Approaches to Tourism

Innovation approaches to tourism provide the potential for a more integrated approach to understanding tourism behaviour. Increasingly sociocultural influences are evident in tourism and arise from societal pressures facing the tourism industry. "Innovation" perspectives on tourism reflect the social embeddedness of the tourism industry. A merger between the innovation and tourism industry research is needed to address the complexity of the tourism industry especially given the recent COVID-19 pandemic. This means changing dominant theories on tourism, so they are updated to include an innovation point of view. This enables more critical analysis to occur that opens our minds to new understandings about tourism processes.

Innovation theories provide an opportunity for tourism researchers to fortify their existing assumptions towards network relationships. The relevance of innovation perspectives (including both an economic and social view) is rooted in the belief that innovation in tourism develops, in part, from the evolutionary forces present in the tourism industry. The development of innovation approaches to tourism over the last decade has dramatically changed research. New insights from this research have impacted decision-making and policy decisions.

People are wanting to discover new experiences that differ from their everyday life. In addition, consumers want more individualised holidays that cater to their needs. In the presence of an uncertain environment, knowledge management is important in tourism. Innovation relies on the availability of knowledge, so any knowledge acquired needs to be managed in a proper way. Knowledge is an asset that can be used to increase a firm's competitive advantage. This means what an organization knows is important but also how they use the knowledge is equally important, which is why tourism marketing is also critical in the competitive success of a region.

Innovative tourism businesses are likely to bring economic gain to their communities. Tourism innovation is a process of new venture creation. It involves the use of risk-taking and futuristic thinking in a business context thereby enabling existing production factors to be utilised in a new way. This creates wealth when aided by collaborative networks. Tourism innovation is an effective strategy that brings about change in a community. The motivation for tourism innovation derives from a multitude of factors including financial gain or social reasons. Organic tourism innovation occurs when a business idea grows naturally and is not influenced by others. However, both organic and non-organic forms of tourism require marketing in order to increase consumer adoption rates.

Tourism research is about studying people's movements and their motivation to travel. Currently the number of innovations based on digital interventions has increased. This has led to a growth in digital-based innovations that are combined with already existing innovations. This includes the use of new sustainable materials or processes that encourage environmental forms of innovation to emerge in the marketplace.

Cultural Tourism

Cultural tourism occurs when people travel to a place in order to experience a culture. Increasingly tourists are wanting to learn something new when travelling. This makes cultural tourism a source of history and knowledge. It enables information about cultural identities and societies to be obtained. Every market consists of different types of customers with specific needs. These customers can be grouped based on their behaviours and motivations. McKercher and Du Cros (2003) suggested that cultural tourists can be classified as serendipitous, purposeful, incidental, casual and sightseeers. Serendipitous cultural tourists visit a cultural place by chance and it is not a planned activity. Purposeful cultural tourists visit a place for a specific reason and the trip is planned. Incidental cultural tourists visit a region because they have gone to another place first. Casual cultural tourists do not have a specific tourist route in mind but instead visit places based on feelings. Sightseeing cultural tourists are more interested in visiting places because of the scenery.

Food Tourism

Food tourism is an important sub-category of tourism and links to cultural pursuits. Due to the different ways food can be prepared and consumed, many individuals are motivated by food tourism. Food is part of the visitor experience and represents an important tourist attraction. There are different forms of food that enhance the tourism experience. Food plays a key role in tourists deciding to visit a place. Food and tourism have a close relationship. This is due to food being an essential part of the tourism experience for many people. The diversity of food available in a region influences the tourism experience. Moreover, niche or cultural forms of food often play a key role in the reason why people travel. Food is vital for human life and is needed whilst travelling. Food can also be a motivator in terms of tasting new delicacies. This means food services as a cultural purpose and offers a source of pleasure. Food also has a social role as a source of entertainment. The way food is made and consumed can provide a source of insight into a community. This helps tourists understand the cultural conditions within a region. Food tourism is called culinary or gastronomy tourism. Trying local cuisines is a source of enjoyment for tourists. This enables them to watch in an indoor or outdoor setting how food is prepared. In addition, tourists can prepare their own food using local ingredients. Special food produced from an area is a souvenir for tourists. This enables others to try new foods and can change a tourists own way of preparing meals. Food is a source of place attachment and can involve emotional feelings.

Surf Tourism

Surfing involves a combination of energy, natural capital and tourism development. Surf tourism is a rapidly expanding market segment. During the last decade, surf tourism as a niche tourism segment has grown due to the interest in surfing as a sport and also regional development activities focussing on surfing as a natural attraction. Surfing is a seaside destination that is subject to fluctuations in the weather and is a popular recreational activity in many beach locations. Surf spots are essential community resources that are available for the use of everyone regardless of income level. Despite the availability of surf spots, there is a risk of environmental degradation and pollution affecting these areas. People depend on surf spots for their social and recreational enjoyment. Moreover, surf spots provide a source of livelihood and cultural identity. Beach areas are prone to development that may lead to an increase in visitor rates. Beaches account for a large number of tourists than other natural and man-made attractions. Surfing is an activity based on nature and the outdoors. It is different to other sports due to the need for the right environmental conditions including wind and waves. Surfers rely on beaches as their focus of activity.

Surf spots are locations close to the shoreline that consistently produce waves. Surfers often develop expert knowledge about these spots due to their frequent visitation to the area. As a result, surfers develop place attachments that act as a source of local identity. Surf sports are not only places where surfing occurs but also a place for social interaction. Whilst surfing is a solitary sport it normally occurs within a group context. Thereby surf spots have a sense of community as others need to share the place. People develop relationships with the landscape that affects their emotional state. This bonding of a person to a place is part of the surfing culture. Each surf spot is unique due to its coastal setting. This means whilst surf sports have the same general recreational purpose that can differ in terms of oceanographic setting. Therefore each surf spot needs to be considered individually in terms of its cultural history and social setting. Surf sports are dynamic as they change based on the ocean environment. This means there is a territorial element to surf sports due to their place attachment. Place identity can be described as the "symbolic importance of a place as a repository for emotions and relationships that give meaning and purpose to life" (Williams & Vaske, 2003, p. 831).

People identify with a place because of its history, location and importance. Surfers are more likely to have more of a sense of place identity due to visiting the location for a long period of time.

Practical Implications

The tourism industry in Oceania is distinctive and needs to be analysed in a different way. Rather than stereotyping all tourism as the same it helps to take a regional perspective. This will enable a better contextual understanding about how culture, society and history have shaped the development of the tourism industry. Tourism practitioners need to also consider context when deciding if and when to be innovative. Not all tourism entities can be innovative as it can take time to develop an innovative mindset. For this reason, thinking about cultural considerations in terms of socio-demographic factors can help determine how the tourism industry can facilitate an innovative mindset. Tourism providers in Oceania need to be competitive in the global marketplace, thus, any advantage they receive from being innovative can result in better performance results.

Theoretical Implications

This chapter suggests that the continued evolution of tourism innovation research needs to re-focus on regional contexts. This will enable new theories to emerge that take advantage of historical and cultural elements within tourism innovation research. As the body of knowledge existing on tourism innovation research is already quite large, new perspectives are needed that enable the research field to continue to grow. As discussed in this chapter, tourism innovation theory can embed a regional context thereby enabling new theoretical frameworks to emerge. This will help in developing new theories that might only apply in specific contexts. Governments of Oceania countries have made tourism a priority industry and recognised its importance to economic growth. In the past, most of the tourists to Oceania tended to come from overseas but this has since changed with an increase in domestic tourists. Over the past decade, the Oceanian tourism sector has grown faster than the average. At the same time, the Oceania region remains one of the most popular tourism destinations and influences the way other countries market their tourism resorts. The tourism industry employs a large percentage of the total workforce and is an important contributor to the economy (Björk & Virtanen, 2005). There is a growing domestic and international demand for tourism in Oceania. In order not to rely on the summer travel season, there has been an emphasis on trying to reduce seasonality by creating other tourist activities particularly related to cultural and sports events. Moreover, the Oceanian government has been emphasising social inclusion in tourism practices in order to diversify their market but also to acknowledge the changing socio-demographic travel patterns of the global community. This is evident not only in the ageing population but also in the increased spending capabilities of older consumers. Moreover, there has been an emphasis on sustainability and environmental practices in tourism. This is shown by governments of countries in Oceania setting environmental standards in terms of water and energy usage in order to preserve the natural environment.

The aim of this chapter is to provide a strategic view about the role of tourism innovation in Oceania. This is useful as the tourism industry is maturing and has radically changed as a result of the COVID-19 pandemic, which means there is an ever-growing range of new types of tourism gaining popularity in the marketplace.

From this chapter emerges several implications for tourism managers, businesses in the tourism ecosystem and policymakers. For tourism managers, it is crucial to emphasize how innovation impacts the outcome of business activities. Tourism businesses are relying on innovation to increase their advantage in the marketplace. This means tourism managers need to take into account the relevance of the innovation when they implement innovation initiatives. To do this means placing value on the innovation, as well as, considering measures that capture the impacts of the innovation. By valuing tourism innovation, it can enhance the reputation of the business. Therefore, mechanisms should be used to manage the innovation as well as introducing ways to share knowledge about the innovative behaviours. For the tourism ecosystem there needs to be more collaboration in order to build synergies. This will enable the tourism innovation successes to be transferred to other stakeholders. In this regard, it is useful to explore the channels that reinforce cooperation. This can occur by analysing tourism innovation strategy where the involvement of innovation is recognised. This can include the implementation of measures that enable the comparison of results with other geographic regions and/or industries. For instance, there are many innovations that occur in the tourism industry that can be translated to other industries. In addition, government policy can have a positive effect on tourism innovation activity. This means additional insights are needed on the best practices or models from the tourism industry that can be replicated.

Future Research Directions for Tourism Innovation

This chapter has described the role of innovation in the tourism context. As discussed, there are numerous ways innovation can be conceptualised and understood from a tourism perspective. This makes it important to take a holistic perspective when analysing any form of tourism innovation. Future research questions include the following:

1. What is the role played by capacities and resources in tourism innovation practices?
2. What influences the development of innovation in tourism relationships?
3. What topics in addition to those in existence in the tourism and innovation sciences are also important to studying tourism innovation?
4. How can existing theories be enriched to explain tourism innovation practices?
5. How might tourism innovation theory be expanded?
6. What potential new content is needed to measure tourism innovation?

Conclusion

This chapter has focussed on the importance of tourism innovation in Oceania by emphasising the role of the tourism industry. This is important to global competitiveness and helps differentiate Oceania from other regional contexts. The way tourism can be innovative was discussed in the chapter. This helps pave the way for more forms of tourism innovation to occur that are particularly important given the recent COVID-19 pandemic.

References

Asero, V., Gozzo, S., & Tomaselli, V. (2016). Building tourism networks through tourist mobility. *Journal of Travel Research, 55*(6), 751–763.

Björk, P., & Virtanen, H. (2005). What tourism project managers need to know about co-operation facilitators. *Scandinavian Journal of Hospitality and Tourism, 5*(3), 212–230.

Caalders, J. (1997). Managing the transition from agriculture to tourism: Analysis of tourism networks in Auvergne. *Managing Leisure, 2*(3), 127–142.

Cassel, S. H., & Pashkevich, A. (2014). World heritage and tourism innovation: Institutional frameworks and local adaptation. *European Planning Studies, 22*(8), 1625–1640.

Chesbrough, H. (2003). The logic of open innovation: Managing intellectual property. *California Management Review, 45*(3), 33–58.

Chung, M. G., Herzberger, A., Frank, K. A., & Liu, J. (2020). International tourism dynamics in a globalized world: A social network analysis approach. *Journal of Travel Research, 59*(3), 387–403.

Cohen, E., & Cohen, S. A. (2012). Current sociological theories and issues in tourism. *Annals of Tourism Research, 39*(4), 2177–2202.

Czakon, W., & Czernek, K. (2016). The role of trust-building mechanisms in entering into network coopetition: The case of tourism networks in Poland. *Industrial Marketing Management, 57*, 64–74.

Dolnicar, S., & Ring, A. (2014). Tourism marketing research: Past, present and future. *Annals of Tourism Research, 47*, 31–47.

Dredge, D. (2006). Policy networks and the local organisation of tourism. *Tourism Management, 27*(2), 269–280.

Edensor, T. (2001). Performing tourism, staging tourism: (Re) producing tourist space and practice. *Tourist Studies, 1*(1), 59–81.

Edwards, J. A., & Llurdés, J. C. (1996). Industrial heritage: Mines and quarries. *Annals of Tourism Research, 23*(2), 341–363.

Feranita, F., Kotlar, J., & De Massis, A. (2017). Collaborative innovation in family firms: Past research, current debates and agenda for future research. *Journal of Family Business Strategy, 8*(3), 137–156.

Gërguri-Rashiti, S., Ramadani, V., Abazi-Alili, H., Dana, L. P., & Ratten, V. (2017). ICT, innovation and firm performance: The transition economies context. *Thunderbird International Business Review, 59*(1), 93–102.

Gibson, L., Lynch, P. A., & Morrison, A. (2005). The local destination tourism network: Development issues. *Tourism and Hospitality Planning & Development, 2*(2), 87–99.

Halme, M. (2001). Learning for sustainable development in tourism networks. *Business Strategy and the Environment, 10*(2), 100–114.

Heiskala, R. (2007). Social innovations: structural and power perspectives. *Social Innovations, Institutional Change and Economic Performance, 1*, 52–79.

Hjalager, A. M. (2009). Cultural tourism innovation systems–the Roskilde festival. *Scandinavian Journal of Hospitality and Tourism, 9*(2–3), 266–287.
Hjalager, A. M. (2010). A review of innovation research in tourism. *Tourism Management, 31*(1), 1–12.
Kahn, K. B. (2018). Understanding innovation. *Business Horizons, 61*(3), 453–460.
Kokkranikal, J., & Morrison, A. (2011). Community networks and sustainable livelihoods in tourism: The role of entrepreneurial innovation. *Tourism Planning & Development, 8*(2), 137–156.
McKercher, B., & Du Cros, H. (2003). Testing a cultural tourism typology. *International Journal of Tourism Research, 5*(1), 45–58.
Morrison, A., Lynch, P., & Johns, N. (2004). International tourism networks. *International Journal of Contemporary Hospitality Management, 16*, 197–202.
Moulin, C., & Boniface, P. (2001). Routeing heritage for tourism: Making heritage and cultural tourism networks for socio-economic development. *International Journal of Heritage Studies, 7*(3), 237–248.
Paget, E., Dimanche, F., & Mounet, J. P. (2010). A tourism innovation case: An actor-network approach. *Annals of Tourism Research, 37*(3), 828–847.
Ramadani, V., Dana, L. P., Ratten, V., & Tahiri, S. (2015). The context of Islamic entrepreneurship and business: Concept, principles and perspectives. *International Journal of Business and Globalisation, 15*(3), 244–261.
Ratten, V. (2011). International sports management: Current trends and future developments. *Thunderbird International Business Review, 53*(6), 679–686.
Ratten, V. (2016). Female entrepreneurship and the role of customer knowledge development, innovation outcome expectations and culture on intentions to start informal business ventures. *International Journal of Entrepreneurship and Small Business, 27*(2–3), 262–272.
Tajeddini, K., & Ratten, V. (2020). The moderating effect of brand orientation on inter-firm market orientation and performance. *Journal of Strategic Marketing, 28*(3), 194–224.
Tajeddini, K., Altinay, L., & Ratten, V. (2017a). Service innovativeness and the structuring of organizations: The moderating roles of learning orientation and inter-functional coordination. *International Journal of Hospitality Management, 65*, 100–114.
Tajeddini, K., Ratten, V., & Denisa, M. (2017b). Female tourism entrepreneurs in Bali, Oceania. *Journal of Hospitality and Tourism Management, 31*, 52–58.

Williams, D. R., & Vaske, J. J. (2003). The measurement of place attachment: Validity and generalizability of a psychometric approach. *Forest Science, 49*(6), 830–840.

Zach, F., & Racherla, P. (2011). Assessing the value of collaborations in tourism networks: A case study of Elkhart County, Indiana. *Journal of Travel & Tourism Marketing, 28*(1), 97–110.

Index

V. Ratten (ed.), *Oceania Entrepreneurship*,
https://doi.org/10.1007/978-981-16-7341-2

The manufacturer's authorised representative in the EU is Springer Nature Customer Service Centre GmbH, Europaplatz 3, 69115 Heidelberg, Germany. If you have any concerns regarding our products, please contact ProductSafety@springernature.com

Printed and bound by CPI Group (UK) Ltd, Croydon, CR0 4YY
30/09/2026
02225260-0018